Sex in 12 Dimensions

Ajani Abdul-Khaliq, PhD

i&R

2020

Sex in 12 Dimensions

First Printing: 2020

ISBN 978-1-7337455-6-7

i&R Publishing
7979 Broadway #209
San Antonio, TX 78209

https://iandrpublishing.wordpress.com

Ordering Information:
Special discounts are available on quantity purchases by corporations, associations, educators, and others. For details, contact the publisher at the above listed address.

Contents

I. Human Forms

II. The Common Dimensions

III. The Uncommon Dimensions

Contents

GUARDIAN'S PREFACE

Before we begin this journey, we'll need for you to make two commitments.

The first commitment: Think about the closest person you have to an intimate partner. You can be married or just friends. In the same house or on the other side of the world. Your age or far from it. They may know about your views of them or not know. Ally or enemy. Socially favored or forbidden to you. Think about the person who is currently in your life right now (or at least on your mind), who is the closest recipient of your romantic affections. If you can't think of anyone, you can substitute a hobby, a calling, or a job. What you CANNOT do is think of someone or something that is not *currently* in your life, who doesn't seem willing to connect to you on your journey, who has died or is not living, or any dream girl or guy who is not actually plugged into your life. They must be within your ability to interact with in a close way, even if it's as an enemy, even if you're not attracted to them physically or otherwise. If they are currently, closely connected to your direction in life, they'll work as a choice.

The second commitment: You must decide to accept everything currently in your life as an extension of your own dynamics. You are a collection of physics—chemicals each with a family of frequencies in their bonds. Your actions exist on a timeline, the trail of your movements forming a ghost upon the Earth's spinning surface. As do the bars of color left by a camera's image in motion blur, your color combination exists in several places at once—events which have occurred and those yet to occur eventually intersecting with you in their own moment of a perceived totality. But you are not real in time…any more than the you from seconds ago is real. Everything around you, everything separate from you, will become you tomorrow—folded into the memory that builds your identity.

This book is for people who are ready to see other worlds. It is not for those looking to improve themselves, to grow, to have better sex, to strengthen their relationships, or to validate worlds already known to them. Only the tolerant need apply. If you're not comfortable with the body and its terminology, if you're closed to partners who don't fit your ego standards, if you believe that love can only be shared with one person—even as you share it with lovers and family at the same time, if you are critical of faiths not your own, if your primary defense against intrusion is argument before understanding, if you are convinced that Heaven can only be had tomorrow rather than right now, this book isn't for you. You'll need to evolve first, then come back later.

We will use the language of many faiths, many identities, and many practices. There will be some science, some psychology, and a lot of spirituality. There will also be one overarching goal:

The intent of this book is to rid you of the desire for experiences you believe you cannot have, and replace all such desires with joy in the experiences you know that you *can* have. We will make you immune to spiritual harm, translate your enemies into friends, and show you the ways in which to be grateful for those events which build your human experience. You must be capable of gratitude. If you are still ungrateful for anything anyone tried to give you from their whole heart, close this book and give it to someone whose heart is more open than yours. Ask them to tell you what they learn from it.

ANALYST'S PREFACE

The writer of this book requested a manual for intercepting the pain inflicted upon a person's self when his or her past difficulties rendered them weak in the face of gifts not requested. Sometimes—actually often—people reject what they don't understand, even if that thing is good. At no time in your recent history has this been truer than in the current age. People believe that when a natural disaster occurs, it is a time to lament material loss rather than forge the true bonds with people they've never met. They believe that death is cause for mourning loss of their conveniently projected fellow man rather than celebrating the opportunity to absorb that fellow man's admired gifts into their own behaviors. People believe that a leader they don't agree with should be spat upon, rather than seeing him as a carrier of millions of burdens, a beacon against the public uncertainty, or at least a reason for those who have always wanted change to finally come together to make that change on their own.

In line with the animal nature of the human body-ship, people still decide their emotional paths on the basis of survival needs long rendered unnecessary. So a human who can't pay his debts believes his life to be equivalent to that of a slave. But no modern human in normal society knows what real slavery is. Only the trafficked. Only the warred upon. We find it strange how men blessed with all they have ever wanted can build lives of suffering upon the idea that some of those blessings are mismatched.

The naked man is without protection. But this clothed man is angry as his blue tie doesn't match his navy pants.

The writer of this book requested a set of instructions for capturing the joy he has learned to acquire through a series of lessons about the world. He sees fortune in the times, and beauty in the enduring guests in life—be they identities, philosophies, skills, or people. Those things that endure—those habits, patterns of interaction, those types of personality, those ideas ever at his side even as material things and people prove fickle: he has learned that all is only an interaction—a section of code on a hard drive full of scratchings, a sampling of waves in a playlist sea within which he swims. To explode the body and realize it as a rippling pattern of characteristic responses, to see that those families of responses constitute the making of form and that such form consists of not much more—this is the secret to multidimensionality.

AUTHOR'S PREFACE

One of the things which has kept me single for a several phases of my life has simply been humanity. As a human, I have a unique set of quirks and have found that the more important those quirks are to you the less likely you are to attract people who will put up with them. Actually, the less likely you are to stably put up with people who don't accept those quirks. And then again, they're not really "quirks" are they? Just the plain old individuality we all have. American society shames us into negatively labeling any trait we might have which deviates from the standard success culture, such that if it isn't fun, outgoing, or status-granting it can't possibly be a thing we want. Especially for those of us whose unique personalities touch on taboo realms, it can be a challenge to find and build relationship spaces which truly allow for our full growth. So we often settle for partners who stimulate us and accept us, and leave much of the rest—like our self-mastery and sense of purpose—to chance. The idea here is that the right partner can lead to that happy ending even if we never get to define happiness on our own. But if we have certain characteristics which defy the socialized standards of partnership, that happy ending will only look like a difficult ending in yours or the other's eyes.

The difficulty for me in relationships has always been the same. On the one hand I want your company; on the other hand, I don't want you taking over my space. I'll serve you to the best of my ability; I'll not be your slave. And then there's that thing about me having goals of my own. We're all good when the relationship is new and everyone's feeling validated, but when we cool off and start turning away from each other (towards our original selves)—when it's no longer about selling the dream to that person you're dating—you say, "So I have this thing I've always been interested in" or "I have this bag of issues I've always been dedicated to resolving," and they say "There, there, that's nice. But getting back to me..." The choice often becomes one of you versus them at that point, and the relationship ends. I suppose the best way to summarize this is that it's easy to outgrow each other as soon as you find out that their lives don't actually revolve around validating you. This is especially true for those of us who hold our own goals in high priority. Including another person into our goals while still making room for theirs can be difficult. No matter how much we may want the companionship, accommodating both sets of ends simply may not happen.

For over a decade I've worked on translating sharp logic into fuzzy human behaviors. Fellow free scholars and I refer to **the extra set of expected behavioral effects that come with a thing** as that thing's **spirit**. We refer to spirits whose effects resemble those of the living as **souls**. The theists among us refer to [the set of rules that compel your optimum chosen expression] as *God*; the atheists among us refer to that same set of rules as *Natural Laws*. The theists—a Christian, two Universalists and two agnostics—seem to prefer translating the principles they follow into chains of human-relevant interactions. The atheists—one Buddhist-Daoist and one nihilist—prefer translating those principles into chains of rational constructs. The theists are generally better at relating to people, but aren't as open to just any people. The atheists are generally better at relating to ideas, but aren't as open to just any idea. And so we go about the business of figuring out life. As the Daoist in the group, my gift is that of codification—the ability to take any pattern, no matter how wild, and present its most natural inner workings as an ordered system. The drawback to this (and it's a major one) is that I'm deathly allergic to interactions whose underlying systems are broken or require work. So I won't generally put in effort to start, maintain, or fix relationships which aren't naturally easy. This goes for people, societal systems, and everything else. If it breaks, I codify it and move on. So every time a promising relationship ends, the result for me is the same: a major breakthrough in my scholarship and personal power. The guardians have something to say about this kind of creation-destruction pattern among people struggling to build good relationships.

First, you already have good relationships. And not all relationships are with other people. Most of the relationships we form are with [groupings of ideas], where the people in our lives represent idea-groups we have outsourced. That is, each person we meet can be thought of as a set of expectations that we hold, set up in fixed packages to respond to our actions dynamically. Related to this, every nonliving object in our lives can be thought of as a set of perspectives we hold—comfortably when it comes to our preferred surroundings—which has an impression-triggering relationship to other perspectives we hold. So,

- **living things** are frozen packages of *processes*,
- **objects** are frozen packages of *outlook*. Additionally,
- **inclinations, feelings, wants**, and **impressions** are frozen packages of *processes whose effects influence the spaces* that experience them.
- **Actions** are *projected packages of process whose forms are determined by the parties that send them.*
- *When an action's form is determined by <u>both</u> the sender and the recipient* (rather than the sender itself), that action becomes a **word / a communication**. It also becomes an outlook <u>between</u> them.

For brevity, actions and other projected processes are called Fire. Words and other projected outlooks are called Air. Objects and other frozen outlooks are called Earth. Feelings and other frozen processes are called Water. Whole collections of all four of these which can interact with other interactors have been called the Spirit element.

A **characteristic pattern of exchanging effects** among all the elements above is called a **relationship**. See how relationships aren't just between objects or people in one dimension, but are really between carriers of multiple dimensions and other such carriers: Spirit to Spirit. We don't have to believe in God or Physics or anything to see this. We only need to recognize that another may appeal to you physically (Earthwise) but anger you in communication (Airwise) and challenge you in action (Firewise). Two object-ideas—like a job and a friend—may appear very different physically (Earthwise), but affect you in very similar ways emotionally (Waterwise). The difference among forms in our lives isn't really in *what* gets offered, but in *how much* of each kind of experience gets offered in proportion and in the order in which those experiences are most easily connected. The difference among songs in music is less about which note frequencies are getting played in a snapshot, and more about the relative arrangement of those notes dynamically. So it is with people and relationships.

How much beauty, how much ugliness? Shown in the body or shown on the ambition? When we form relationships we are choosing to interact with this much charm in this particular form, and this much security in that particular form. Sometimes Earth objects exchanging Air words constitute the best relationship forms for the job we wish to perform as Spirit packages. Other times, these relationship forms are not so desirable. You might find it interesting to note however that even when traditional human relationship *forms* aren't very good for building the best kinds of human relationship-associated experiences (like Water happiness), they are always good for something. For the author of this book, human relationship forms are better for studying more than anything else, certain kinds of disappointment are better for peaceful isolation, and peaceful isolation is better for *actual* human relationships. Likewise, some people need war before they marry. Others need to lack security. By knowing the self's patterns we gain the ability to choose where we park on the patterned property of our personalities. From there we invite others to represent certain perspectives for us, just as we invite certain environments to properly frame those perspectives against the greater attitude towards our universal Rule Set (God or Natural Law). All in all, our views of Self, Other, and World mirror our views of our own instinctual pattern making, the interactants and places we immediately exchange with, and the Rule Set/God/Natural Law which circumscribes those immediate exchanges

<Self, Other, World> as forms = <Instincts, Interactions, Rules> as processes

Whenever we assign forms to things, we are telling life "Please freeze that as a package for me to do things against—even if it's just a reminder." Some Self forms, like our physical appearance and our general way with words, are comparatively difficult to change because they constitute our lens for viewing everything else. Without these as they are, we'd lose a large part of our "plot line" for living life's movie. Other forms, like our families and work patterns are changeable, but serve to remind us of the "genre" our life's movie belongs to. Because they are so instrumental to human identity—and are often the only reflections we can rely on before coming to know ourselves—we don't typically change those we consider family—until after we've owned, then disowned certain trained aspects of the lives we started. World forms are analogous. These are more easily changeable reflections of the communities (film eras) with which our life movie is associated. We may move from place to place, travel temporarily, or connect to a foreign locale, but only after we have owned then disowned certain views of the Rule Set we follow will life see fit to move us easily.

So Self, Other, and World are our means of freezing our dynamics with our own basic Instincts, patterned Interactions, and next-step Rule Sets between any two experiences of any kind. Call these the three scopes. Meanwhile, we can think of things as packages of **projected processes** (actions, **Fire**), **projected perspectives** (communications, **Air**), **frozen processes** (feelings, **Water**), and **frozen perspectives** (fixed forms, **Earth**). Attaching each of the three scopes onto the four kinds of element, we get 12 dimensions over which relationships may unfold. When I interact with you, I'm not just parading a body around (Other-Earth), I'm also relating to a pattern of personality (Other-Fire), a type of co-communicator (Other-Air), a set of internal ideas about what you represent to me (Self-Air), and eight other dimensions of experience ranging from a kind of object that I validate in the world (World-Earth) to a kind of impression I leave on whole environments when I arrive with you (World-Water). Many a relationship has been ruined because the participants have not appreciated the non-obvious dimensions—like having a person who keeps the other's broader dreams alive (World-Water)—until it's too late.

Many people assume that the great goal in life is to find happiness. And this isn't a bad assumption. But happiness in what? Happiness with oneself (Self)? One's accomplishments (Other-Earth)? One's surroundings (World)? Even if it is happiness with oneself, as an internal psychology (Self-Air)? As an identity (Self-Earth)? As one who wants for nothing emotionally (Self-Water)? This is why rich societies are in particularly good positions to foster multi-level happiness among their citizens beyond material status. While some societies dream of grand prosperity, rich societies know that such prosperity goes far beyond the narrowly material. Through discontentment with their vast Earthly acquisitions, they begin to see the value of emotional harmony, lives without needless pain and oppression, and systems open to experience of things once feared as foreign. So it is with people. Humans strive for the status advertised to them by those who claim to possess the means to such status. Prior to achieving those status objects, we feel as though we are living in scarcity. This is as true for money as it is for quality relationships. Having acquired the things advertised to us, we then realize that what we wanted was less a function of those things and more a function of our own relationships to…whatever we chose to relate to at any moment. There in Self-riches we see: Our Others and our Worlds are the fulfilled person's playground.

That's what the Guardians said about that.

Who are the Guardians and Guiding Spirits?

As a Buddhist-Daoist, I believe that no form has form but for the exchanges it has with other patterns not like it. For me this means that humans like Abraham Lincoln don't just exist as bodies (especially not now on November 17, 2018), but also exist as associations in the broader mind—even after their bodies are no longer active. Lincoln is considered to have been a physical Earth form, but to his parents he was once a psychological, Airy possibility. To us he is a historical memory, as well as referential relative of ideas like the Civil War, assassination, and Union. Where memories and impressions like these fuel our next actions in whatever context we're in, Abraham Lincoln becomes not only a historical structure (World-Earth), but a social mood-trigger (World-Water). When we get into the realm of things leaving effects despite their absence, we enter the realm of spirits. In this example, Lincoln's spirit is associated with the Civil War and emancipation, while his soul—the living-like behavioral pattern which summarizes his spirit's effects on our actions—can be summarized as "One who battles against the division that drives war." **If a thing has a standard effect on the average viewer despite its absence, that effect is its spirit (definition 2).** If that spirit seems to change its behavior towards you when you change your behavior towards it, and if the type of response it gives is pretty standard to all interactors, then that spirit might be described as having a stable, human-like personality. Then we can refer to it as a "soul" [definition 2]. Abraham Lincoln's spirit probably wouldn't think it was cool for us to chain up a slave. That spirit-preference for having an opinion (in our eyes) makes it easier for us to talk about Lincoln as having a soul.

Given the above as a starting point, we can think of any pattern of events, any pattern of wants or compulsions which 1) [favor our benefit] and 2) [follow us around] as being "spirits" associated with us. One of my colleagues refers to hers as *guides* because (obviously) they give her guidance. I refer to mine as *guardians* because I tend to frame things I like in terms of system structure and strategy. So my word for them has more of a kingdom-based or state-institutional feel. Spirits which remind you of your forebears might be called *ancestors*, and spirits concerned primarily with your Rule Set might be called *angels*.

Unless we have psychological problems, we're almost always doing something towards our own benefit—even if it's just scratching an itch. Even if it's helping others. That's not to say that we always prioritize such self-benefit over everything else, just that there is a potential for self-benefit that can be found in every next move we make. Accordingly, I believe most of us always have guardians hanging around. The stronger the awareness of what benefits us in a particular area, and the more you are able to frame that benefit in terms of a personality like yours, the stronger the guardian.

The better we are at separating that which benefits us from that which doesn't in a particular area, and the more able we are to interact with that separation as if it had a personality, the clearer the communication with the guardian. The personalities of your guardians are based on how you feel when you're engaging them. Because the ideal solution for almost everything is the solution which promotes the most harmony for mostly everyone, I've found that guardians are far less likely to judge or talk smack about your "enemy" than you are. For everyone's best ending, the guardians tend to be really easygoing (or at least broadly beneficial by definition).

And why do you care about this?

Because throughout this book I'll often reference my guardians and write what they tell me. This is my way of saying, "Though I may not know you as a reader, the feeling beyond myself which I get that might benefit you is..."

To build relationships with others beyond the standard ways of perceiving, we can start by taking inspiration from beyond our standard modes of perceiving. Paying attention to the World-Mood around you is one way. Observing the Other-Inclinations of things you pick up is another way. You too have guardians. And as long as you don't adopt ongoing personality exchanges with information around you that promotes *damaged* interactions with Others, you can have guardians without having demons. Your guardians exist for your benefit. By their nature, they message you best when you are open to feedback from the non-tangible aspects of things. We'll need this in order to connect strongly in the other dimensions we talked about earlier.

On Sex and Airspace

As a technical astrologer I've encountered all kinds of topics, but few have fascinated me more than the connection between passion and the intellect. To compress a long story here, I struggled for a long time trying to understand why passion and intellect seemed to go hand-in-hand with me—why I couldn't have one without the other and, in situations where I needed to use one I would always get the other. Part of this comes with the territory as a Scorpio Sun, but the other part of it comes from a general parallel between sex and research: Both involve taking a thing and laying it bare, a cycle of mutually influencing the other's expression played out between you and it, as well as (for some) the need to go where few others are allowed to go. In general, if I'm not passionate about it I won't study it. And if it doesn't receive my intellectual side, I can't get passionate about it no matter how alluring it is. If the terrain is full of arrogance, problem-dredging, or needless criticality I'll drop it for friendlier topics. If it boxes me in using standards I shouldn't have to relate to, or would prefer me to morph into somebody else just to get "published" I'll tend to treat it however I feel, pressure it to take a final stand, then be done with the trouble of it either way. Some of these are seen as bad habits, but only when I put myself in what we'll call **irresonant relationships**: exchanges which don't easily match your natural personality. When you seek an outlet for your passions, you often seek a World-Mood of intensity. Bad results are normal when that outlet is only a tool for some other experience. And though I, like you, don't consciously use people for my own validation needs, I often do this *subconsciously* as a result of failing to claim the real reason why I enter relationships: Personally, I do it for the study. Then I write books like this for other people in the world. In the end, through passion comes creation. This is a theme we'll turn to over and over again throughout the book:

Sex = Creativity

Who you do it with and how. Who you're not doing it with physically but are all in with communicatively. Why you do it emotionally with people you think you hate and why it pays to forgive them after you've killed each other off. These are all topics we'll address. If the name of the game is happiness in whatever form you seek it, then our task is to lay out those forms for your choosing.

Why Focus on Sex

Surveying the currently advertised American terrain, I've noticed something. Relationships are everywhere. Good relationships are easy to create. We have great relationships with friends on various media outlets, with our favorite shows as identity anchors, with our homes and cars as experience objects. Relationships aren't where the difficulty lies. *Deep relationships*—most specifically the relationships to *ourselves* as actors in the world—are where the real challenge lies.

Under a strongly interconnected society, we now have the ability to restrict each other as never before. If I am outraged over something then I am free to say so out loud. If I think something is gross or inappropriate then I can shame the culprit publicly. Because it only takes one disgruntled voice to uncritically knock down another without hearing the latter's backstory, we all operate in a society where anything non-standard, defiant of the public pressures, or uniquely different can get effectively squashed by only a fractional number of naysayers. As a result, our social networks, though apparently large, also expose us to fr&nds whose values aren't really ours, but whose lifestyles and secondary networks challenge our own sense of what's acceptable. So having 300 connections on social media but three true friends in real life helps me carry—if I'm not certain of my individuality—297 question marks over how I've chosen to live into my relationships with those three. It was hard enough getting three people to accept my true secrets even before I plugged into the web. Now I have constant reminders of who I'm not. As for my true friends and partners, sometimes they're really deep. Most of the time they're deep enough to provide me with sanctuary from everywhere else, but not deep enough to help me evolve past where I am. They may even need me to stay where I am as a means to their own safety. And what is lost is the ability to open up my truest self for further development. My closest friends are fine, but it would sure be nice if I had someone who would advance my real dreams, to stay with me—judgment-free—as I work out my issues, and with whom I would be equally interested in co-evolving.

As with guardians, there are some experience patterns which show up easily as other personalities in our lives. These people, pets, plants (or whatever) do things in the world on our behalf where we wouldn't have the internal setup to do those same things as easily ourselves. It contributes to their useful purpose, and we continually do the same for them. Unless you live completely in your head, you will outsource things—clothes to keep you warm instead of having your metabolism do it, a home to house your identity instead of having your head recreate that identity every morning. A mother to remind you of what you are challenged to overcome, a father to remind you of what you could become. A pet to draw out your caretaking pattern, a partner to be your communicative reflection. These are things we outsource. The deepest among these, however, are those people who not only serve as our mirror, but who co-create impressions for us to leave on the broader world. Those typically qualified to be full partners can do this 1) without rank problems, 2) without engagement limits, and 3) in a way that is tangible and observable. So 1) normatively-restricted relationships, 2) systems, and 3) abstract ideas don't *usually* work for this kind of thing. (But as we'll see, perhaps they should.) Ideally our partner-mirrors love us and we love them. They may create long-term offspring with us—human or ideologically—or share our most private affairs in the world. In a socially tangled society, intimate co-creative support is easier to seek for safety reasons rather than for intimacy reasons, and can be harder to perfect against the backdrop of collective opinion. We'll focus on sex because we have a lot of work to do in destigmatizing the toolset available to deep psychologies; sex and the analogs to it are about as deep as it gets for plugging you fully into the others that matter. And the self that matters.

About This Book

Sex in 12 Dimensions is an adult book. I will talk about pussies and dicks and vibrators, grannies, fetishes, and masturbation. I'll also talk about how things like this might relate to you. I won't use politically correct words where gonzo words would do because, honestly, a chapter that discusses the sex through art should feel like a chapter about sex and art. Not about research. I will, however, tone it down when the need arises.

More than anything, I'll talk about forms. Body forms as perceptual triggers. Social forms as assumption writers. Psychological forms as interaction pavers. As in basic physics, we'll assume that no solid form is truly solid, but is an energy carrier full of empty space. No solid dick is truly solid, but will be an energy carrier full of empty space (eventually). For every act we engage in, every experience we have, every body part or object we bring into our plans to fuck somebody, there is a family of actions, communications, feelings, and implied physical correlates that come with it. The sum of these dimensions shapes the next state we and our partners experience, so that finding deep fulfillment becomes an exercise in aligning ourselves with a moment—more than aligning ourselves with a physical body.

If I could state one goal for *S12*, it would be for you to discover two rules for yourself: one for describing the things you create in the world and the other for describing who you create it with. I am a system structurer who co-creates with rare artists. You will be whatever you are, and a co-creator with whomever you preferably partner with. The rules won't be a narrow as they sound and when you find yours you'll see that they can applied broadly no matter where you are. They'll work whether you're sexin', painting, watching TV, or all of the above at the same time. Most importantly, they'll help you clarify the kinds of things your Spirit should and shouldn't stand for. So a happy couple may not need this book for intimacy, but they can use it for experimentation, insight into other people around them, and clarity on how to best co-create in, say, their jobs or their life goals. Once we've gone through the various dynamics, the forms will be easy to swap out.

Okay, now that' we've laid out the terrain, let's get started.

I.

Human Forms

1 SAY I LOVE YOU

This chapter is not about sex. I know you might want to skip it. But if you do, you may find that lots of things in the rest of the book won't work for you. If you're going to explore other dimensions with your partner you'll need to be open. This chapter will discuss how to unlock those doors so you can receive intimacy from wherever it comes.

Back in college I had a roommate whom I got along with very well. We talked about a lot of philosophical topics, and one of those topics was the ability to say I love you. The roommate, a heterosexual male like me, agreed that there was something oppressive about the societal taboo against a male being able to say "I love you" to another male without putting their sexuality on the line. And given that our conversations were often deep and insightful, we were able to exchange the occasional I love you until our stay at school ended. The passage of those three words wasn't very often, but it was meaningful when it happened; I didn't realize how meaningful it was until a couple of years ago when I heard it said among Superbowl champions. And this year when I heard again among Superbowl champions. Apparently "I love you" is a thing among romantic partners, not a thing among fr&nds. More than fr&nds, it's a thing amongst close friends, not a thing among everyday males protecting their macho-ness. More than everyday males, it becomes acceptable again among conquering teammates and comrades in arms.

The end result: the acceptability of "I love you" depends on when and how it's used. We get that part. But now here's where trouble begins:

While "I love you" is acceptable among people known to be close, it can spell the death of relationships which have been intentionally placed at arm's length. Women don't like hearing those three little words from men they've "friend-zoned." Men don't like hearing it from women they consider unattractive. Colleagues usually aren't supposed to say it to colleagues even if the relationship is close enough to warrant it. And you generally shouldn't say it to someone who is married or otherwise attached. Why? Because when you say I love you, there is an automatic context attached to it.

I love you like family.

I love you like a deep and true friend.

I love you romantically.

These are the basic three. And where our society really celebrates sex while hiding intimacy, we assume that if it's not the first two it must be the third. But if I've friend-zoned you, you're not allowed to use the third one or do things that make me *think* you're using the third one. I've killed several platonic-looking relationships by crossing that very line. I say "platonic-looking" though because by the time I've gotten to this point in a clearly questionable relationship I've already concluded that the other person isn't really interested in my company, but in her own validation. There, I've sent an I love you (or an I love you-looking act) of the 4th or 5th kind (listed below), and let the exchange put itself out of its misery. Only if the other person responds considerately to your honest expression (or at least seeks clarification) should you continue to deal with them. If they disrespect you, cut you down, or stand on a pedestal—if they hear one version of what you said and raise the alarms, without checking to see if they heard correctly—then you know: this is skewed communication we're dealing with, where your Other might be one who chronically hears what they want. Maybe the two of you can endure in some ways. But it won't be in *every* way. Someday, maybe not today, you'll turn toward the exit. On that day you'll remember how they boxed you in from the beginning.

Because they couldn't receive what you gave, only what they heard.

"I love you" is valuable in our society not just for bonding with others, but for sampling another person's defenses against further connection. Since I often hang out in spiritual circles, I hear "I love you" all the time, and it usually isn't romantic. When it has been romantic AND come from someone who by social prescription shouldn't have said it, my default has been to get over the initial awkward feeling and keep a respectful exchange going anyway. This is partly because of how I was raised, and also because I never know the next time I will be in the confessor's shoes. To judge them out loud or in my mind is to set a precedent for how I think I should be judged when I show interest in somebody. Maybe they'll never know what I think. But I'll know. And this gets us to the heart of "I love you" and why it's our starting point for traveling the 12 dimensions.

People who knock you down when you bring them goodness are almost always insecure. With themselves, with their accomplishments, with their responsibilities, reputation, or whatever. There are things they want which they have—in their minds—failed to achieve, and judgment is their weapon of choice for putting perceived failures "in their place." Said another way, those who judge others also have Failure as one of their bedfellows. Even if they own three mansions and happen to frequent the talk show circuit, those who judge must live with the shadow of potential failure more than a poor person who doesn't judge others. This is especially true of those who knock down others who attempt to give them good. When that happens, Failure doesn't even have to arrive. Not Being Good Enough is a still more enduring nuisance. Now maybe you haven't observed this yourself. Maybe your world is different from this. But I've observed it in decades worth of people I've known, and in the relationships worth paying close attention to, it has happened EVERY TIME.

> Critical Judgment of [others] and the Fear of Failure in [oneself] go hand in hand.

> Critical Judgment of others' honest, best efforts and the feeling of Not Being Good Enough also go hand in hand.

We may be searching for the deepest love. But when it's given to us by someone we don't want, how do we treat them? We don't have to love them back, but do we respond to them in a way that still respects them?

A Love for Each Dimension

I have a basic definition of love which I have sworn by for over a decade:

Love – a feeling of ongoing harmony in light of the thought of a thing

In love with – a feeling of ongoing harmony in light the thought of what you receive from a thing (experience-wise)

Whenever I need to ask myself whether I really love someone, I ask whether either of the above applies. If they do, it might be romantic or bonded love. If not, other kinds of love may still apply.

In order to make it safer for ourselves to give and receive love in dimensions other than the physical-romantic, it helps to outline some forms of love other than the familiar three. Now, since I'm an astrologer, I'm going to attach signs which correspond roughly to the 12 dimensions mainly because those signs (if you know anything about astrology) are more descriptive in this case than phrases like "World-Earth" or "Self-Water." Let's take a look.

Type of Love	Dimension	Related Sign	What It Is
Popular three			
Legacy (family)	**Self-Air** The kind of love you announce to family members and people you're stuck with, whether or not you have any active feelings attached to it.	Gemini	I love you, mom.
Bonded (deep friend)	**Self-Water** Love in one of its deepest senses; the kind where you feel stably connected to someone on your shared path through life. Does not need additional action on yours or their part.	Cancer	There is no one I trust and connect with more than you. It doesn't have to be romantic, but I'd do anything for you.
Romantic	**Other-Water** Love mixed with the desire to influence the loved thing's actions in your favor (or get them to influence yours).	Scorpio	I'm passionately invested in you. Come to me babe.
Other kinds of love			
Liking	**Self-Fire** Harmonious feeling that applies while something is being experienced, not necessarily afterwards. (By the earlier definition, this isn't really love because it's not enduring as a feeling. Still, we use the word "love" to describe this all the time.)	Aries	He's one cool dude. I love that guy.

Type of Love	Dimension	Related Sign	What It Is
Self-Esteem	**Self-Earth** Love that comes from your identity or sense of self being associated with something	Taurus	I love you, my beautiful Rolls Royce.
Stage	**Other-Fire** Love of expressing yourself to others, often along with the love of receiving their feedback in return	Leo	*The crowd cheers* I luh dis shit.
Dedication	**Other-Earth** Love that comes in association with an interacting object or situation	Virgo	I love you, my afternoon gardening.
Apprecia-tion (of Company)	**Other-Air** Feeling of deep connection in light of a special or uniquely rich exchange	Libra	This conversation we just had was so great, I feel...I mean I wish I could tell you how great it was. I'll never forget it.
Spotlight	**World-Fire** Love of a persona you've projected onto the larger world	Sagittar-ius	Look at what I just did. I am such a badass.
Comrade	**World-Earth** Loves that comes with an irreplaceable status given a shared event with another	Capricorn	We made it through deployment together. I love these guys.
Collective (Honor)	**World-Air** Love of the greater context which houses other, smaller elements	Aquarius	I love my country. I love Christianity.
Setting	**World-Water** Love of a setting or environment	Pisces	I love this song (which typically means you love the experience of this song as it plays).

Now suppose an acquaintance of yours in whom you're not romantically interested confesses that they love you. What do you do? You can do whatever you want, BUT

> Unless you've completely found the happiness you're looking for in all of the above dimensions, you might at least consider being kind to that person.

The confessor is an actor in your world. If you put them out with a snicker, in their eyes you are probably selfish. A common thought they might have is, *You've probably done this before and you'll probably do it again. No wonder you're unhappy. See how far your selfishness takes you when someone else has something you want—especially if that something happens to be access to your own dream relationship.*

There are plenty of forms of love to go around. Get used to receiving it when it's given to you. Boundaries are still okay. But you don't have to be a jerk.

As I got more comfortable with hearing the three little words from people in all sorts of contexts, a couple of things happened. Angry people started disappearing from my life. And when I heard the words, even though I may not have been interested in the person romantically, I often valued them in other ways. To return the sentiment but still be clear, I'd say things like "I love you too. I'm not really in a place to commit, but I really like our talks" or "Oh, thanks. So when's the next time we meet?" Granted, these may be dodges, but a dodge is sometimes easier on the relationship than a cold no. It is true that sometimes a cold no is warranted. But a lot of the time it isn't. Especially for people with a pattern of destroyed relationships, a gentler dodge might be just the thing.

Anyway, in the world of sex and love, never say never. You may dodge them today, but next year you may miss their genuine desire to chase you. Or maybe you'll actually miss them.

What Do You Actually Want?

Let's end this chapter with a discussion of want. Suppose you're looking for greater fulfillment in your life. Someone offers you love (or at least support), but you're not really comfortable taking them up on the offer. As is very often the case, however, the person or situation which offered support to you is DEFINITELY related to the fulfillment you're seeking. Are you honest with them about where you see them? Do you sugarcoat the matter, keep them at a distance, and keep them around until you reach your goal? Is there some other solution?

Again, you'll do whatever suits you. But you may notice that situations like this pose less and less of a dilemma the happier you are with yourself. When I was younger, situations like this would vex me. As I've gotten older and much more secure, I simply ask what it is I actually want.

Want – A person wants what they turn their actions towards the experience of

Given the above you can ask, "Why has this situation come up? Did I want this person to do this?"

We often want to keep people at arm's length while at the same time enjoying the ego high of imagining they want to jump our bones (even if they don't). In that case, I might actually *want* you to hit on me even though you're beneath my standard. And I definitely plan to reject you once you do hit on me. That's the subconscious for ya. In this example it's all about me bolstering my ego at your expense. But to ask what I really want...Is *that* what I want? Knowing the answer is yes, I can almost certainly find better and more long-lasting ways to inflate my ego *with* your cooperation than against. You are, after all, my groupie. If I really wanted to trip you in front of an oncoming car I would have done so by now. So even if I AM using you for my ego, destroying your dreams doesn't have to be part of my plan. We could just as easily double date: me and someone who's not you...with you and someone who's not me.

Take the honest love given to you. Borrow a fake sweetheart if you need to discourage the romantic kind. But don't be mean. Defensiveness will only lock you out of deeper sides of your own world.

Remember:

- If someone offers you goodness, consider taking it! It's possible to receive a gift but keep boundaries at the same time.
- If you can't accept someone's love, intentions, and so on, try not to be a jerk when you tell them no. Being mean sets you up to be followed around by various insecurities later on when you put *yourself* in a position to be judged.
- If you're not sure you whether you want something, ask yourself "Regardless of what my mind thinks, are my <u>actions</u> steering me towards this?" Before you shoot the messenger offering you candy, check to see if it was you who invited the delivery.

2 ON THE FORMS

Think fast. When you have enjoyable sex, what kinds of physical things are involved? (Turn to the next page once you've thought about it.)

Bodies? That's probably a given.

Toys? For some, maybe.

Condoms, lube and other such supplies? Okay, gotcha.

How about the stereo or TV?

Food and other spreadables, perhaps? Now we're getting kinky.

I'll bet some people forgot to list clothing—what stays on, what comes off, and when. Isn't that part of the whole mood?

What about the setting? The bed, the couch, the shower or (my personal favorite) the kitchen counter. That way I can grab a snack when I'm done. Then again, maybe you prefer the plain ole floor. Doin' it rustic-like.

The overall ambience, the room you're in, whether you prefer home or a straight up MO-tel. These all count as tangibles.

What we note here is that sex isn't just about bodies slapping. You probably wouldn't try some of those fancy tricks on your neighbor's porch. Privacy matters. But an empty white room with a stone slab in the middle may not do it for you either. Certain decorations and a sense of comfort are important. (Turn that picture of grandma around if you don't want her winking at your flopping junk.) The physical environment consists of everything that creates the setting, plus the people. And although many of the extra objects may not play active roles in your memory of the scene, taken together they'll likely play a collective role in making the setting what it is. In this way, Earthy physical objects act less like objects and more like Watery feeling-creators.

More on that later.

Next, think about *how* you have sex. How do you behave? Take a moment to list it somewhere. To help you along, take special note of whether you are any of the following:

- Quiet, loud, or somewhere in between
- Active, passive, or somewhere in between
- Server or served
- A talker
- Animalistic or reserved
- Full of extra enticements or basic get-down
- Lastly, note what kinds of things you tend to think about before, during, and after sex. This one is extra important.

As you can imagine, people behave in all kinds of ways during sex. What's interesting is that those ways strongly resemble their creative processes in everyday, non-sexual arenas. This is especially true of how they think during the act. One might guess that all people think about various forms of pleasure during sex. But you probably know better. Some think about children. Some truly think about love. Others think about bills. I usually think about places I haven't visited yet, in a process that looks suspiciously like my programming and policy-writing work. A technical approach to the partner for a technical approach to institutions. A poetic experience for a poetic mind. An animalistic experience for a spontaneously dirty personality. These are examples of how Fiery actions during sex have Airy mental equivalents in the non-sexual setting.

Finally, let's turn away from sex for a moment and think about how you perform your daily duties at work. Specifically, what do you do when you're bored and need to release your boredom for something more pleasurable?

- Do you talk to others? Go around and visit them?
- Do you text people, hunting for interaction?
- Do you get up and leave?
- When you're feeling caged in, what do you do?

Your spontaneous remedy for boredom is related to your Self-Fire acts, and shows your basic instinct for freedom. Whatever you do and wherever you go, these have implications for the conditions you set up for your own creativity and, by extension, the sexual situations you prefer. For example, when I'm really bored, I vanish from the office and can't be found anywhere. I go where there are no people, no computers, no voices, nothing. It may not surprise you that I prefer immersion during sex—where the partners and the settings merge into the same blank space. In a case like that, it's not that the white room with the stone slab does it for me, but everything has to match; the music, the time of day, the room, and everything have to go together or else I'll get irritated. I'm also quiet as a mouse during the whole thing. That's my preferred set up. And although the advertised lore (at least to males) is that a man should be able to smash it anywhere, it just doesn't have to be that way for everyone.

Using the space below, take a moment to describe your boredom behavior. Think about your preferred settings for sex and how these might be related to such boredom.

Let's review:

- Earth physical objects can be transformed into Water mood-creators
- Fiery sexual behaviors have Airy mental equivalents
- Self-Fire boredom behavior translates into World-Water preferred sexual settings

The examples above show us how the forms of things can change depending on the situations we put ourselves in.

There are things we attempt to create and things we are masters at creating. Most of us don't know what we're masters at, but can find out with a little help from our partners. Before we describe how to do it, though, let's discuss the topic of forms.

The Role of Forms

We're all familiar with at least three of the basic states of matter: solid, liquid and gas. Taking water as an example, solids remain contained within their own shape boundaries, liquids flow within an externally defined set of boundaries, and gases expand to fill their external boundaries, but don't flow in the same way as liquids. The states of matter are determined by a combination of the energy put into them, the pressure they're subjected to, and the volume they're intended to fill given their density. Our various life circumstances can be thought of in a similar way. The pressure to be exciting is heavier on a date than at work. The density of emotions is heavier in a fight than in a peaceful park. The energy put into your performance of duty is heavier when the bill is due than when you're being treated to lunch by the boss. And although you have the potential to do any of the things that you have ever done already and will do in the future, you won't necessarily do them in the same proportion unless the conditions say so.

You can fight, sleep, or work, but on the job it's work x 10, sleep x 0.1. At home it's sleep x 8, work x 1. Depending on where you do something—and whether the situation favors your doing it, the same activity can be very healthy (sleeping at home) or very risky (sleeping on the job). While you're at home, sleep may take the form of an actual Fire activity in the very beginning and at the very end while you're half awake, but when you're out cold, sleep becomes a Water state where dreamland and body repair take over. You may not be able to do this at work, but you can have a kind of half-sleep where you space out for a while. An example might be zombie-mode where you let the blogs sail by your eyes as you appear to do real work. Here, sleep becomes a very passive version of Air.

So we can sleep in various ways, but the broad patterns we follow for doing so will still flow into a more general psychological blueprint for "restoring energy." This is a kind of state change where the form taken by sleep can shift depending on how coherent you are in engaging your situation. Is there a way to turn physical sleep in to a kind of Earthy object? Sure, just record yourself during the process or have someone take a picture of you. It may not be a live capture, but it will produce a tangible representation of this otherwise experiential process.

Shifting forms is a fundamental skill for intentionally attracting good, multi-dimensional relationships. In fact, is it the single most important skill for attracting a good partner or major life change in general. On "form shifting," the guardians say this:

You always have everything you need, including those things needed to build an optimal life. While most people throughout the human ages have shifted forms accidentally, you are entering the era where it is possible to easily shift on purpose. For example, a man can easily turn his dream job into his dream partner. A woman can easily turn her child into a great work of art for the rest of the world to marvel at. If only these individuals would recognize the parallel feelings they had for small things, and apply those feelings towards greater things.

Suppose, for example, a woman seeks a successful and loving partner. She is approached by many successful men that do not truly love her, but only seek her as an object. At the same time, she is loved deeply by her pet and her child. Still she is lonely. What can she do? Showing gratitude for all involved, she should begin to build her world around the happiness brought by the pet and child, that their fortunes may multiply. She should also be grateful for her own value, seeing the unwanted men who approach her as proof of that value. Lastly, she should refuse to invest energy in active dissatisfaction with any of these. If the men are of low quality it is better to look past them than to look at them angrily. With these strategies in mind, she will engineer what we call a "merge"—where separate chapters in a person's life combine into one. The key to a form shift like this lies in the woman's attitude towards those who bring her unwanted or underappreciated gifts.

In previous times, men relied on their own efforts to generate novel outcomes. This is because most systems were almost entirely controlled by men who valued the exertion of active power towards any worthwhile end. As society has changed to a more rumor-based culture, it is much more important to be nice to everyone you meet. There are some downsides to this, but in terms of human effort it is a grand improvement over previous times. For people in more developed countries, social approval is more about having a positive and accepting attitude, or at least a charming one. Thus in order to bring about change in one's life all that needs to be done, about half the time, is that the individual change how he or she treats her interactants. There is no real need to do things that you don't want, only to stop doing things that you know *others* don't want. If you are habitually mean towards certain things that continually benefit you or are habitually dismissive of things that provide you with nothing but opportunity, you will either go blind to those opportunities in the long term or will capitalize on them to your own detriment—rising higher and higher until the height of your fall is much higher than it would have been had you never risen at all. Such is the end reward for one who stands on other's backs. He or she may be the grand ruler throughout much of this life, but on their deathbed, those who were dismissed will eagerly wait to divide up the legacy and commit the ruler's name to history's shame list. That is how a rumor-based society works.

The author of this book was told that he needed to write it before he would be allowed to see the rest of the world in full. He asked us why. The reason is because, in the current society, there is no greater remedy for humanity's ills than the individual's ability to love as many as he can, as openly as he can. People in a prosperous republic continually complain about their government, but they don't know what a tyrannical authoritarian regime looks like. People in a tyrannical authoritarian regime complain about their government, but they don't know what a war-torn nation marred by genocide looks like. Because a comparatively free people do not know how to love their jobs, their institutions, and each other the way they love their lovers, they believe that all of those other experiences are subpar. At the same time, many of those same people do not know or love themselves. And so they rely on their physically-embodied human romantic partners to carry the former's definition for them. The author of this book was told that, as a fairly lusty, but still disciplined individual, he would know both the value of open passion as well as the role it must play as a dilution to human's tendency to impassioned warfare.

Love is easier than hate, even if hate for that which one doesn't know is the more popular path.

A book about sex and sexual relationships is necessary not for the lessons in physicality it provides, but for the exercises in transcendence that have to be explained in order to convey those lessons. Pleasure is but one of the aims of sex. Bonding is another. Belonging is another. Security is another. A sense of control is an aim. So is a sense of order amidst chaos. All sex is creative of an experience which is typically rarer to the participants than other kinds of creation, and in that sense all sex presents an opportunity for the participants to bring their full instinctual ingenuity to bear. When sex becomes routine, lacking, or unavailable in a soul who really wants it, then the opportunities for sharing of this potentially beautiful unfolding are also capped. Through form shifting, even happily partnered humans learn to see new avenues in their individual creative options, leading to the same kinds of discovery as an artist experimenting with a new medium.

So ends the lesson.

When I asked about the secrets to easy form shifting, the guardians told me, "Take everything towards which you have a negative attitude and consider yourself its writer. Especially things that have done nothing but bless you." I also received a hint that the United States was one of these things. Although it's not necessarily the case that our country has to jump into the bed with us, our attitudes towards the various identities involved in the country's events are related to our attitudes towards the kinds of people we'll date, the ways in which we fight back or feel we don't matter, the friend groups we join and solidarity they possess, and the extent to which we're willing to plug in to other's struggles. For easy relationships we need easy surroundings. For openness to our own untapped spaces we need openness to certain things we once feared as foreign. For security in our partnerships we need strength in the protections we provide *for* our partners. Although changing an event from a Watery feeling to an Airy communication is easy, it may not be pleasant if your communicative world is filled with chaos. The reason it's often simpler to continue with business as usual is because business as usual is typically more familiar, and (at least *feels*) safer. But if you should ever come to see the familiar as a kind of cage, know that escaping that cage may require you to get on better terms with the world outside of that cage. In this way, the wrong country, the wrong city, or even the wrong family can mess up you and your partner's expectations for each other in ways you've never even thought of. To change attitude, our task is to see as much right with these things as possible, and plug into outlets aimed at improving everything else. Negativity and negative friends will only weigh you down (and really isn't very sexy either.)

I guess the moral of the story is that you can turn a perfect interaction into a perfect partner, a perfect favorite movie into a perfect creative hobby if you know how to shift forms. Shifting forms consists of taking your attitude towards one kind of experience (like Watery emotions) and applying it towards your behavior in another kind of experience (like an Earthy object). But when you do this, be sure your outlook in the new kind of experience is one that serves you. Otherwise you may get more than you bargained for. Unlike places of employment, people are very dynamic, have continuously changing behaviors, and will demand that you respond as them as uniquely special individuals. If you were to develop a person-like love for your dream job and transform it into a dream partner, keep in mind that you'll also need to adjust to how this person treats others, views new things, and supports you. It has been suggested that our views of government are often impaired, and this affects our appreciation of the systems that sustain us. If we attempt a form shift which involves institutions we hate, we may attract something we hate. Duh. Staying as positive as possible towards as many aspects of our lives as possible allows us to shift across several of the 12 dimensions without problems—including the more World-centered dimensions.

Maintaining the Shift for the Long Term

Most form shifts are temporary unless we truly renounce something, or adopt something, or make a permanent relationship-altering move. Before I ended my last exchange, I learned this lesson through meditation and decided to try it out on a person whom I had stopped trusting a couple of days prior. The idea was, if you want to seriously change something in your life, you'll need to make a move which leaves permanent effects. This seems to be a very useful rule of thumb when you're trying to generate new life events from old ones. Finally posting that article, finally telling that guy how you feel about him, finally selling that painful stuff—each of these can constitute a permanent act which can change your world forever.

Given the above, we can now talk about the kinds of steps needed to attract a kind of ideal partner if you don't already have one. If you do already have one this won't apply to you, though you may find it interesting.

The guardians say this regarding ideal partners:

First of all, we assume that you've already heard it said many times before: One should determine whether she even needs a partner before attempting to attract one. Except for the truly spiritually injured, the best partner is almost always oneself. We assume you've heard that. A good test to see if a partner would help or harm you is to look at the most important thing you're currently doing in your life and ask if the any of the kinds of people around you can support that effort. Can they make you better in that effort? If the answer is no then you probably don't need a partner unless you want to learn a kind of karmic lesson (the hard way) related to the relationship between others and this most important thing.

If you can tolerate being unpartnered while you work on this thing, you might ask your guides for help before inviting someone who will only get in your way.

If you do decide that partnership will help you focus your most important efforts better, the next thing you should ask is, "Is there anyone or anything around me for whom I would give up my current path for a shared journey with them?" If the answer is no and you obtain a partner anyway, don't be surprised if your partnership is falls into distance or conflict over one person not trying hard enough. If you knew you weren't willing to share your path with this person before you entered the partnership, but only sought them for more utilitarian reasons, don't be surprised if the partnership is less than ideal. If the answer is yes and you are willing to share paths, then a partner might work for you.

There are several other questions you can ask regarding whether you need a partner, but most people who want one will simply go out and get one, if for no other reason than the validation it affords. As for an ideal partner, there are two more questions we can skip to:

1. **Is there anything in my life which I consider persistently, happily ideal?** If yes, you at least have one of the ingredients for an ideal partner. If no, then you may not recognize an ideal partner even if they rang your doorbell; ingratitude for the ideal things you do have, unwillingness to look at things which try to be ideal to you, and cruel judgment of anyone or anything striving to be ideal in their own way will prevent you from achieving a real ideal. Even if you meet the perfect love of your life out of sheer determination, there will be other chapters of your life which will ensure your dissatisfaction stays with you throughout that partnership.
2. **Do I *want* an ideal partner? Am I turning my actions towards attaining one?** A no speaks for itself. A yes should be considered alongside the previous question.

Now, some people like the author *would* seek an ideal partner, but consistently answer no on the above question 2 because they do not believe in the selection of people generally available to them. Maybe they think a partner would chain them, interfere with work, or obligate them to strange family and friends-in-law. In cases like this, partners may not be ideal, but might be needed simply as a bridge to new aspects of those things which the person really values. Maybe you don't seek an ideal partner because that person would impede your bachelor lifestyle. But if your bachelor path requires that you be a bachelor in another country, you may inherit a partner to take you there. This is where one attracts partners that are not ideal in themselves, but ideal for the shared work created— what we'll call *provoli filia*. The rules for attracting a person like this are the same as the rules for attracting an ideal partner in their own right, except that eventual separation is almost guaranteed unless the needs of the arrangement change during the chaperoned transition—usually a very brief window of weeks if the meeting times mainly with the move instead of timing on a schedule long enough for a genuine relationship to form. That is, ideal partners whose purpose is to advance one's work usually enter and leave quickly.

To attract an ideal partner, one must do three things which are only easy to those whose attitudes are sufficiently trainable:

- Amplify the thing currently in your life which is ideal everyday
- Refuse to mistreat or otherwise underappreciate anything which has the qualities you want in your ideal partner. If you want your partner to be confident but dismiss confident people as stupid and arrogant, you may attract somebody, but they likely won't be ideal.
- Know your own purpose in life, and ensure that the above two factors align with it

Although we'd like to like to tell you that ideal partners can exist for you while you have yet to know ideals within yourself, it's more like these are "idealized" partners rather than "ideal." It's hard to build a wedding cake out of nails, so if you don't know your own purpose, rely on someone else to define your purpose for you, or simply don't accept your own talents, the partner you attract will only reflect your own need for an anchor. They may monopolize your life or simply direct it, but as the embodiment of a soul you will be their subject. If they are the kind of person who is okay with this, then perhaps an ideal can be achieved after all, but truly unbalanced relationships born of incomplete evolution rather than adult preference are rarely satisfying for both parties in the long run.

The author of this book asks whether there is any way to know where to look for an ideal partner. Our answer is, "Anywhere." Just as a certain note can appear in two different songs at two very different progression points, deeply resonant energies will cross oceans years before the physical people decide to look for each other. There is usually no need to travel unless doing so is part of at least one person's journey, and meeting on the journey is part of at least one person's experiential plan.

We would like to close this chapter on form shifting by re-emphasizing a key theme. To transform one part of your life into another form, you'll need to have a reasonably healthy attitude towards the form you're transferring to. Ideals can't be easily built on shaky, negative foundations, but require your best attempts at gratitude towards the various characteristics that constitute that ideal. Besides this, form shifting is all about mapping your contented approach to one situation onto another. The less you judge and dismiss small things, the more you tend to them—especially as analogs to the things that satisfy you but for their differing form—the more likely those small things will grow into great things nurtured by your appreciation.

End of lesson.

3 WHY WE HAVE BODIES

This chapter consists of the transcript from one of my guardian channels. It was in response to a question I asked, *Why do we have bodies?*

1

Through the example of war, we see at least five or six answers to the question of why humans have bodies. First of all, there's the notion of class—whether it's nationality or political membership (that is, being the citizen of a country), whether it is the notion of ethnicity, or even sex. **Class belonging** is one the reasons why humans have bodies.

2

Another reason why humans have bodies is **physical movement**. Things like dance, things like battle, the use of swords and guns and other kinds of weaponry, the movement of fingers on the piano, the way people walk, the way people sound—these can broadly be described as movements. Note that mannerism is part of it too.

3

The third reason that people have bodies is **to interface with other classes**. To use the sense to touch things, to be able to hear certain sounds—just the ability to interface with other kinds of experiences. You don't get this as easily when you're not embodied. You just get intentions. Intentions are great; it actually makes the spirits more powerful than the man. However, the spirit doesn't do nearly as much in terms of detailed high-resolution expression. An example of this would be a video game.

4

You can spend two hours playing a video game and really feel the same kind of amused feeling [the whole time as the player], but your character will have killed 200-300 bad guys, walked all over the map, leveled up, gotten hit, drank healing potions, gathered forces, and done so many more things than you would have done as his spirit and frankly experienced more, really as a reflection of the first three issues: Movement, class, and the senses. So another one of the reasons we have bodies is for **high resolution, dense experiences**, the fourth reason.

5

The fifth reason why we have bodies has to do with aging. You may not think aging is an important part of the human process, but it really is. What does a thing do at the beginning of its life versus the end of its life? What does it do at the beginning of its intent versus the end of its intent? The aging process is the process of an intention reflecting from its most youthful, most nascent state, when few people believe it, to its mature state when everybody knows that it has reached the sum of its expression. Some people die young, and their ways of reflecting intent never get past youth. People like James Dean or Marvin Gaye die young or at least die seeming young, and that's because they are associated with characteristics that only go so far. It turns out that the aging process is partly controlled by the intention that you live for. Some people say that it's health and whether you smoke or drink, but that's not really it. It's more about the class of attitude that you promote. If you're all about youth and rebellion, and you never intend to change, you may die at an age where your relative youth will capture the spirit of your rebellion. If you're all about a kind of an innocuous class which never really asserts maturity over anyone, then you'll be popularly remembered, at least, in your prime. This is how someone like Audrey Hepburn is. We're not going to remember the older version.

But then again, if you're someone who does assert that kind of authority—that kind of mature power to command—then you may manifest it in one way as a youth but in a different way as you get older. This is Brigitte Bardot. People reflect packages of intent, but they also reflect lessons that were meant for other people. And the span of their lives is essentially the span of their usefulness as an intent. Some people are meant to just serve the intentions of the parents in the raising process. For example, [the author] had a childhood classmate who died before high school graduation, and that's because his intention as a soul was for the experience of his family, the experience of his parents. And then of course you have children who die very very young, some even stillborn. Their whole point as an intention is to guide the parents through a particular phase of interacting with themselves and with each other. The age at which an individual dies tells you something about the intention that they reflect as a soul. There are people like [the author] who don't live extra long lives because those who live extra long lives are more of a testament to the longevity of a thing, and that tends to be associated with family-based intentions. It tends to be an indication of how long the individual served as a kind of reference point for the family. People who live past 100 and actually age accordingly (though this will be extended in the future)—people who live so long that multiple generations can continue to gather around them and point to them and reference all that they lived through, are really there as historical and familial reference points. And if you're not that, then you don't typically need to live this long.

So if you are a typical scientist, if you are a builder of systems, or a constructor of social dynamics or socialized meaning, you'll tend to live the second longest kind of period. These are people in their 80s and their 90s. These people are better as indicators of social systems, but they don't stay around so long that stable families can point to them because that's not what they're here for. They are meant to capture ideas—abstract ideas. But those who live into their 100s are here for more coherent ideas—the basis of the family. And so you'll get people who die in their 70s and 80s—the Einsteins of the world. And you may ask, why don't they live to be 100? The reason is because when you live past a certain number of generations, you may have to change original nature of the science you worked on to match the new sciences of later generations. It's really not that efficient for scientists to do this. It's like having an age where cars evolve into planes. You may have been an expert car mechanic but at some point the cycle of invention is going to turn all cars into flying cars and maybe you can adjust, but there will be an evolutionary line at which flying cars are no longer cars, they're basically planes and you have to ask yourself whether you're going to be a good "plane theorist." But if you're a good plane theorist, your contributions to the science of cars will be lost. And you won't be known as a famous mechanic. You'll be known as a famous "transportationist" broadly, but that actually takes away from the salience of your contribution. And this is not just the case with scientists, it is also the case with those of any kind of cycle length attached to them. They live long enough for the information associated with their life contribution to be captured, but they don't live so long as to make their life phase go into something else.

And so you'll have babies who die because their intention was to reflect a certain necessary dynamic among the parents

You'll have young children who die because their intent was to reflect what the parents are to do in light of a creation that never came to maturity.

You'll have young people who die because their intention is to reflect a kind of friendship dynamic among those left behind.

[Additional examples omitted here.]

Now when we say "their intention," it's more like the intent that they represent. It's not the *individual's* motive to do these things. It is the individual's package that they represent. The lifespan of an individual body is a fundamental part of why that body is here.

Intentions have to be realized at some point, otherwise they only exist in the realm of potential—at least in the realm of potential with respect to those who know a certain kind of reality. So there may be a realm in which things which are immortal in the human dimension are actually mortal in their own dimension. Mountains are like this. Mountains are effectively immortal in the human dimension. But in the cosmic and Earth dimensions, mountains are very mortal. They evolve just like people. In any event, the fifth and probably (we think) the most profound reason that humans have bodies is for the process of **aging**.

Aging is the process that spans the window where you as an individual get crystallized. If you don't age, you're not real. If you were created, you can be and probably will be destroyed. Even the higher spirits work this way. But as individuals we find that part of your reason for being on this Earth is tied up in how others will have perceived you after your intent has been completely realized. Why do humans have bodies then? Humans have bodies in order to reflect a package of intent by the overall cosmos itself (and we can shorten that and call it God or the Great Spirit). But the overall world has to have certain things that coherently manifest. In order to achieve that coherence, those things have to manifest in full. You wouldn't use words, for example, that never end. If we have words that never end, we have ideas that never become coherent ideas, and that actually flies in the face of why we have bodies in the first place. Bodies constrain us. They constrain us to class, they constrain us to a certain pattern of movement. They constrain us to a certain preference for other people's classes. They constrain us to a certain span of senses, and they also constrain us to a certain style of intent which eventually has to have its window capped in order to be completely expressed. That plays out mainly through age.

6

The sixth reason humans have bodies has to do with **multidimensionality** and that's because the systems beneath you have a need to assemble and the systems above you have the need to mature and make order of themselves. If you want an analogy to this just think about yourself as a body. The systems beneath you include organs which have been put together using your DNA which have assembled to form you. The systems above you like cities and states need citizens, they need people in order to interact; they've matured socially, historically, and politically, and their engine of expression is you.

This is why humans have bodies.

II.

The Common Dimensions

4 DIMENSION 8: *Classic Sex*

Surely you already know. One of the secrets to great sex is great communication. Another secret is that of relaxation—at least in terms of the pressures you put on yourself and your partner. People need to be into it, of course. A third secret to great sex is openness—not only to a certain set of experiences sponsored by your partner, but also to a certain style of feedback given to you by your partner.

- Communicate (Air)
- Relax and follow your instincts (Fire)
- Open up to the partner (Water)
- Open up to your own body wants (Earth)

If you have these then you and your partner are ready to go. Easy right?

We'll describe classic sex—the get down and screw version—as **Dimension 8: (Normal) Sex**. It's the first kind we'll talk about

37

because it's what most of us think of whenever the topic of sex comes up. Dimension 8 corresponds to **Other-Water**. That is, the kind of exchange where you focus on steering the **other** person's **feelings**, or steering their next actions based on your feelings. Although the dimensions don't need numbers, from here on I will be numbering them according to the astrological sign they roughly correspond to. Normal sex corresponds to the 8th sign, Scorpio—the sign also associated with death, the occult, psychology, research, and any place where you influence your interactants in ways not visible to most. Here we're using physical actions to tap into deep emotions, so that one person plays the game on the deepest level possible in another.

Classic sex is typically an emotional affair, and is often measured in terms of the level of pleasure or release it brings. Where individuals are certainly free to pleasure themselves, sex brings the added benefits that come with bonding, acceptance, being appreciated, and a relatively safe route into the unknown. Where normally people don't venture off into the unknown unless they're prepared, sex allows us the chance to lose ourselves completely in the capable hands of another. There are countless ways to have sex and countless paths to the four "secrets" listed above. So what is there to talk about here?

Despite the socially pressured ideal, I'll bet you didn't know that not all people are looking for great sex. Or maybe you did know that. Whatever the case, "greatness" in normal sex is typically a measure of the amount of pleasure or enjoyment that one person gets at the hands of another. Yet some people's Other-driven pleasure isn't always physical. Even when it is physical, it may not be via another naked body. By chat or by phone, through power wielded over another, via vengeance or make up sex, through ritual, the macabre or the shedding of tears, the kinds of things that constitute pleasure-triggers even in classic sex are at least as numerous as the number of types of entertainment out there. So when we get in the bed for the first time with someone, the standard expectation is that Body-A will stimulate Body-B and vice versa using, of course, their bodies. It's the reason they held off for the bedroom scenario in the first place. But that's not always necessary, even if Other-Water *is* what you're looking for. Instead, anything that another person does which can get you hot—positively or negatively—can work if you're willing to play along with them.

Ever since I was in high school, I noticed a biological quirk of mine: I'm turned on by making a girl cry. Not through abuse and not on purpose, but when I've done something that really hurts them and it bothers me to see them hurt, the turn on is automatic. Now our American society might suggest that this was pathological, that I need to be repaired somehow or at least get medicated. But no, I'm perfectly healthy. Those of you who know your fetishes might call it dacryphilia. But nope. I've checked out some of the crying-fetish videos and they don't work for me. More than anything, I just wanted to take this feature of my biology and investigate it. The conclusion was that, psychologically, I like to know that I can affect my partner emotionally. If I have no proof of this outside of the bedroom I'm much less enthusiastic about having sex with them in the first place. Relatedly, you probably wouldn't be surprised to find that in non-sexual settings, I never take on a challenge unless I know I can win. As it is in the bed, so it is out of it. Classic sex may be fine the first few times with a new partner, but like all pleasures it can become routine for at least one partner. When it does, adding "spice" might help or might not. A better bet would be to engage your partner the way any object subject to their one-on-one power would. Let me give you an example.

> Stacy loves to win in business. She likes to see the other company's guy squirm when she makes a brilliant counteroffer, but she doesn't get much out of dealings with noobs. Her husband Anthony is a contractor who loves to see a job well done, doesn't like sloppiness in his workers, but tends to discipline them with a fairly gentle hand. Both Stacy and Anthony are pretty intense people, and in the beginning their sex life was excellent. Now it's more about having it when Stacy wants, and Anthony only wanting it when he's been frustrated with his day. Anthony clearly has his mind on

other things, and Stacy can't excite him the way she used to. What's wrong?

The last part was a trick question. We can't tell what's wrong based on the above, but if Stacy and Anthony communicate, *they* might be able to uncover the issue. Note that this is an issue (compared to where they were at least), but not necessarily a "problem." If something really is on Anthony's mind, that something may live in any of the other 11 dimensions we've yet to discuss. It could be work. It could be his aspirations. It could be her. Or maybe it's him. Based on the above, though, we might guess some things about how to help restore both people's reduced pleasure from the Other.

Given Stacy's profile, she might be less fulfilled by a "noob." Since Anthony is her husband, it might be less about experience and more about how he used to be all in, but now is less so. Here it's the drop in engagement that matters. If only Anthony seemed more into the sport of it, only to end up being conquered by her yet again (in yet another new way), she might have an easier time with him as subject to her power.

Anthony's disciplinary style was described as fairly gentle, so that a partner subject to his emotional influence might be more pleasing if she let herself be coaxed into a more "perfect" experience. His and Stacy's power styles seem to differ enough that Stacy's naturally competitive way might hinder this kind of sex, and this may even be compounded by Anthony's feeling that he is not doing a good job in the sexual setting. Perfectionists who know they are imperfect behave in all kinds of ways. Stacy might help him by being tractable in the bed, but someone who is detaching the way Anthony is probably needs solutions for his mind, not for his body.

Dimension 8 As a Pattern

So much of classic sex is psychological. Where the time we spend with each other physically can certainly be fulfilling, that time is rarely a substitute for the rest of the ways in which we have to *live* with each other. Whether we've become bored, preoccupied, or just uninterested in the other person, there typically remain ways outside of sex which can still get us feeling as though we've completely bent that [whatever it is] to our will. The person who behaves like that [whatever it is] towards you, and gives you access to their bodies as a way of letting you do your thing, has a better chance of being an enjoyably classic sex partner than one who doesn't. Of course they'd have to get to know your influencing-power wants in the first place. It also helps if they're interested in helping you fulfill them. Not just in being fulfilled themselves, and not simply judging you for having them.

Remember:

Classic Sex is a deep version of the same preferences partners have for successfully bending things to their will in non-sexual spaces. If you listen for these preferences and take on the role of the things your partner loves to influence, good classic sex will be a breeze for you.

Discussing Dimension 8 With Your Partner

Have your partner complete these three sentences:

> **The situation that makes me feel powerful over an interactant:** When I'm [doing] _____, there's nothing that won't do what I want it to do. (This situation makes me feel like a boss.)

> **The kind of power holder I would cooperate with:** I would definitely let myself be puppeted by _____ if I were personally asked to be so. (This doesn't have to be a person, but could be a situation)

> **The kind of power-subject who would cooperate with me:** I love feeling like a complete master at influencing [this kind of

thing, person, or situation] _____. (This thing loves "following my orders.")

These questions are all about where the other person feels they have a strong power to move the things they interact with. And now, one more:

Turn off: Whenever I'm [in this situation] _____ I feel like I'm being robbed of my power. If I never had to do it again, I'd be alright.

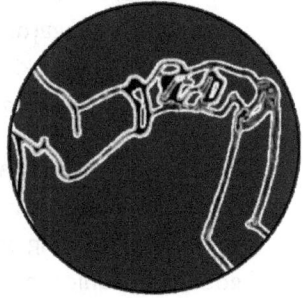

5 DIMENSION 7: *Lovemaking and Intimacy*

For some people, bending another body to your will is just too much work. Why should I be responsible for your pleasure? You know what you want, YOU take care of it. But maybe I still enjoy your company a lot. Maybe I even love you. So much so that it doesn't matter how much you do to satisfy my power needs. All I want is to keep this exchange between us going.

Whether a great conversation between two people plays out through words or through traded physicality, the aim of the Other-Air exchange is for those involved with it to willingly give their next responses to acts just performed by another person. In a true conversation, we never really know what the Other will say or do next, but continue to engage them based on whatever that may be until the occasion reaches its end. **Lovemaking and intimacy, Dimension 7**, comprise an ongoing loop between or among the actors, and differs from classic sex in the sense that the goal is continued participation in another's shared responses to you. Classic sex revolves around the feelings you both feel at the hands of the other. If sex is a sports matchup, lovemaking is a dance.

Some people find that Dimension 7 and Dimension 8 are tough to combine with a partner who isn't patient. If you and your partner have ever differed in your preferred pacing for physical sex, there's a good chance it may have been because one wanted it hot and heavy while the other wanted to take it slower. Somewhere between wanting to receive more of another's company and wanting that other to stimulate you regardless of the company, lovemaking and intimacy yield to sex and fucking, so that their gifts and your wish list can crowd each other out through mismatched pacing alone.

Now it's not actually necessary to separate power wants from communicative sharing if you and your partner are aligned enough in your understanding of each other's needs. This is the standard plug for good communication that we've all heard, but in this case the communication gets extended past what they want from you, past what they seek to do themselves, and into how they draw experiences that are NOT you into the picture.

We tend to look for the signs instinctually. Certain sounds the Other makes or the words they use. Changes in breathing. What they touch or what they guide you to touch. How deep in the zone they seem to be. What they tell you to do or how they want you to move. Some of these signals are part of the conversation between you. Others are part of the monologue with themselves. And while there's no need to get too wrapped up in details that will surely vary from partner to partner, there is something worth nothing about the signs one gives in intimacy.

First let's consider **intimacy** to be something like **your level of engagement with a person's deep wants**. They can reveal their deep wants to you, but if you're not engaged with them, we won't consider this intimacy. You can be engaged with the person, but if what they reveal to you remains shallow, we won't consider this intimacy either.

Perhaps you've met people who were hot for you, but revealed almost nothing about their wants when you (as appropriate) asked to know. Perhaps you've met people who told you their life story, but didn't seem to respond to you attraction-wise. Now that we have two dimensions for comparing, we also have a chance to start seriously discussing compatibility. Where one person likes to grind it down and the other loves to float the wave, we can see where—in some cases, not all—these two might not be as sexually compatible as the ideal would call for.

Just as Other-Water sex preferences can be partly seen in how you use power on the things you interact with, Other-Air sex preferences can be seen in the substance of your great conversations. Remember that "great conversation..." example for Libra in the "I Love You" chapter? In what cases does a conversation—or a conversation-like behavioral loop—strike you as exciting? Is it during social night with friends? Playing music with the band? During a philosophical one-on-one? Sternly with another over a chess board? Where the feedback flows, and each person's next move is an adjustment made to someone else's previous move, we have a conversation—using words or otherwise. Willingly entering those conversations, without needing to steer either them or yourself emotionally, takes you out of the realm of Scorpio sex and into the realm of Libra lovemaking.

Perhaps you've heard of lovemaking as an art, and there is something to this. If the creation of art involves an ongoing check by the artist between what she has made so far and that which exists in her envisioning, then lovemaking can be thought of as an ongoing translation of the moves of another into the broadly blissful experience of the partners' time together. Listening is a key part of it, but not intrusively so. Deep feeling is often a part of it, but mainly towards the process of our continued giving, and giving again to another. From what we have in inexhaustible supply, not from what we want in unquenchable thirst. So there is also a natural connection between lovemaking and beauty, where **beauty describes the object whose perception invites the viewer to continue perceiving, in**

pleasurable harmony, in the way that she currently does—a perception that reinforces itself based upon the preferences of the viewer rather than terms applied to the view. To the extent that a person allows herself to fall into an experience and swirl around in it for a while—to do so without deconstructing it or placing demands on it, she can allow her continued view of it to produce the next phase of the experience for her. And there we have still another connection not just between lovemaking and beauty, but between beauty and appreciation, where this kind of Other-Air engagement relies strongly on the ability to appreciate the scene-defining role played by the partner. Classic sex doesn't require this.

Can you make love to someone you don't appreciate, or have a great conversation with someone you won't listen to? Anything is possible. But in general, Other-Air sex depends on listening to what the partner tells you. Not just hearing what you want to hear. If the latter describes you in your partner's eyes, even the gentlest-seeming sex won't cover up the cage you've left them in.

A Fact-finding Exercise

Take a moment to think about a couple of situations where your exchange with others was absolutely blissful—where there was such a synergy between you and them that you just didn't want to leave. Preferably, this memory won't be sexual since sexual memories will introduce emotional effects we're not looking at right now. Pick at least two memories like this.

Describe those memories to yourself. For some real insight, take a break from this book, get a pen and paper, and write these memories down. We're going to take a look at this description and get some facts about you from it. It's very important that your description not change once you see the next page. (For data gathering purposes, if you're up to it, you may want to write down several such experiences. When I did it, I wrote down six. A sentence or two is more than enough.)

Dimension 7: Lovemaking

Your great conversation memories may be dense or sparse, but they will usually have some common elements. Some of these elements may include

- The type of person you were involved with
- The type of situation
- The setting
- The topic
- The family of feelings you felt
- Your age or life circumstances at the time

The common themes in your scenes tell you A LOT about where intimacy and lovemaking come easily for you. My list looked like this:

- *V and I sharing a pizza on a gray day at school, before she introduced me to the actors*
- *L, J and I on a beach at night, watching the waves, reading astro charts, and drinking a bunch of Sylvaner at a café afterwards*
- *S and I sitting on the floor outside the classroom door talking about her hopes for the future, with the mean girls around the corner.*
- *A, B and I one evening over an assignment to music chosen by B, art done by A, and me as the lead.*
- *M and I working on a puzzle together in total silence at the office on a quiet, partly cloudy day*

In all my memories, the common themes were 1) dealing with someone who was as much of a loner as I was, 2) the overall environment—especially the weather, 3) art and artistic environments, 4) a sober, yet idealistic topic (a conversation between dreamers), and 5) the existence of a third person or thing that we bonded over. The communication in these settings was spectacular in my book, and indeed supported my aversion to super social butterflies, environments that don't match, artlessly busy settings, small-talk, and strict one-on-ones where deep intimacy is concerned.

How about your list? Did you learn anything interesting from it? **Remember:**

- Where intimacy comes easily to you is where you are more likely to feel listened to.
- Beyond lovemaking, knowing where you have great conversations is also useful for knowing what kinds of friends best serve you. If your friends don't have qualities that resemble those common to your list, you may be keeping them for other reasons besides great idea exchange.

I once had a partner who expected Dimension 8 sex from me before I figured out that this wasn't my style. Instead, Dimension 8 power-wielding is the mode I use to do research, not sex. Our association failed as I spent years trying to recover my self-esteem from her and her continued comparisons between me and other dudes, but I ultimately learned some very positive lessons from it. Some people's paces are just mismatched. You never need to change yourself for anyone. But until you take the time to learn your own style, you'll continue to struggle under the unfitting styles demanded of you by others. If you're not happy with the person others are asking you to be, but you don't know why, your challenge is to learn who you are. Simply saying "I don't like that role" isn't good enough. Knowing your intimacy preferences is one way to truly begin drawing that line in the sand, not just for the kind of lovemaking you gravitate towards, but for the kinds of conversations you accept in general. Take some time to look at how you prefer to be listened to, and as you grow, start distancing yourself from people, bosses, businesses, information sources, and other things that don't do this. You don't need partners who make you feel voiceless. And you don't need to give your energy to places that do the same.

6 DIMENSION 1: *Rule-less Fucking*

Fucking is for the uninhibited. For people who like to keep tight
<u>control</u> over how they're seen (especially by their partners), fucking
may not for you. That is, unless the person you're fucking lets you play
out your control in some other way. Sometimes a fellow gets so horny
he doesn't care how you feel. Sometimes a woman gets so horny she'll
go for the pants drop in public. Yes sir. The last of the three well-
known kinds of physical sex, fucking is the mode least concerned with
closeness, most concerned with release from constraint.

[My guardians stopped me here.]

This chapter will be the shortest of all, because in reality it isn't really
feasible to fully release your animal instincts on another unless you
have some kind of brain problem. Instead, what we commonly
describe as the **primally uninhibited fuck** is actually a pretty
well-controlled—albeit extreme—form of normal Dimension 8 sex.

And even though many of us are taught to think of **Dimension 1** sex as the very definition of great sex, Dimension 1—to the extent that it consists of *complete* spontaneity—is actually closer to the "nasty" kind than the great kind. For any of you more conservative readers who would never do piss, bukkake, exhibitionist gang bang, bruising, or ceaseless laughter, the kinds of things people do when even moderately uninhibited will put the average couple's mere bedpost shaking to shame. It doesn't take much to fuck hard and pile on the @#$! words, if that's what your measure of great sex is. All it requires is a partner who will let you go animal on it.

Completely unrestrained sex needs two things: one partner who is ready to be a temporary object and another who is ready to treat the first person like an object. What they do doesn't always need to be scandalous, but where there is a need for something that goes past either person's emotions (Dimension 8) or communication (Dimension 7), there's often at least some temptation flout sanity in favor of something mind-numbingly drastic.

To be honest, I was actually prepared to write a full-length chapter on Dimension 1 and what it's associated with in a person, but my guardians stopped me and essentially said, *Don't spend too much time on this one because many people will have been taught to privilege this kind of sex above all others, and that's not good.* They went on to say that although it is very easy to have this kind of sex given a willing partner, living too long in Dimension 1 at the expense of any of the other 11 dimensions is a sure road to a degraded sense of self. I asked why. They said because favoring this kind of sex above others is similar to slamming cats against the wall for a hobby. It's not really emotionally healthy for anyone, but buries the person's reasons for needing that release beneath a band-aid. Hard sex is one thing. Asking someone to completely let their instincts loose on you is another. One might say, "Of course that's not what we do!" But the message was, even in moderate forms, the habit of agreeing to be each other's thrash object introduces issues of limits that those same people wouldn't want to touch inside their own subconscious. Any issues they might have related to being "worthy" or "good enough" for example would remain turbulently tangled.

If you're looking for a good approximation of Dimension 1 sex, you'll need a partner who will accept even your most extreme habits. Or you'll need to *be* a partner who would accept the extreme habits of another and be able to get enjoyment from it. Sex like this is more about the opportunity to exercise a broad instinct than it is about either person's specific makeup, so hopefully you'll keep at least some Other-Air or Other-Water alongside this Self-Fire package. Few people ever reach such extremes as to completely damage themselves through continued objectification, but it has happened. Hopefully you and your partner can reach some understanding outside of the sex as to how best to proceed.

Being an object for another's inner savage can be fun. But don't hurt yourself swearing by it.

That's it for the three familiar kinds of sex. And now for the good stuff.

III.

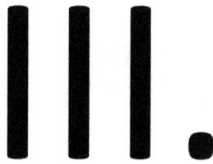

The Uncommon Dimensions

7 BODY PARTS

Before we get into the next 9 dimensions, we'll need to open another door for you. While we typically seek happiness in different areas of our lives, we're very often incapable of knowing what happiness feels like in those areas. A person may seek his dream job, but be unable to feel joy in work as he knows it. A person may seek security in her life, but only know how to feel insecure in her encounters. In order to grab a thing you've sought, it helps to know what it looks like or feels like. But people often neglect to train feelings of contentment, even though those are exactly the feelings they want life to simply hand to them! In this chapter we're going to take a close look at one aspect of a person which essentially remains with them from birth till death, and that is the body. There's no room for shame here. Your body is your announcement to the world telling that world how to behave around you. We'll assume that your soul chose it. And if you don't believe in a soul we'll assume that your DNA chose it, your psychology was influenced by your DNA, and if you haven't gone out of your way to change it, your psychology at least chose to frame things against it. The aim of this chapter is to lay out the different sides of that announcement to the world so that, regardless of how you initially felt about yourself before reading, hopefully by the end you'll have a better basis for owning and feeling pleasure in what you have. You'll need that sense of ownership for the remaining nine dimensions.

Stature, Biological Sex, Skin Color, and Dress

Stature, sex, skin color, and dress are the first impressions we get of you from a great distance. Only dress is easily changeable. Stature comes in two forms: how tall against the norm and how big against the norm. But what a person considers normal will vary *widely*. Still, some people have a stature that is undeniable. Stature (height and weight) affects people's assumptions about your ability to command others' actions.

Height

- **Tall** people are easily seen in a crowd and command attention when they make moves, they elicit others' cooperation more easily than the norm, and are more likely to intimidate those who have to pass through them for something.
- **Short** people are also easily seen in a crowd, though less than tall people. Unlike tall people, a short person's accomplishments are more likely to be attributed to the strength of their personality rather than being assumed connected to their tallness (or that default charisma / command which we assign others who are tall as a way of discouraging ourselves from challenging them). As former cavepeople, we like physically tall folks because it's safer than not liking them. But the reason we don't pick on short people is often because they display *actions* or mannerisms that suggest we step off. A lot of this effect will depend on the shorter person's resting face and race as we come closer to them. And that's the benefit of being shorter. People have to make their assumptions based on *actual encounters* with you.

Being tall helps those assumptions get formed by default. This is also why tall people really do seem to have more of a cool about them. Decisions regarding them can be made from far away, so they don't need a bunch of folks coming up close checking them out like zoo animals.

- **Normal** height people discourage both distant assumptions about their abilities with respect to others as well as close approach of people who are only dabbling in the personality space. The advantage of having normal height is that people must approach you for you, not for your ability to beat out or influence others. If you're a soul who would prefer to attract people for [who you are] and not for [what you can do] in the world of others, having normal height is a good bet.

As with all traits we can have mixtures of height. I'm 5'9". That's statistically normal, shorter than the average black or white American male, but taller than the average Hispanic male in my base city of San Antonio. In terms of accomplishment-seeking, does that mean other blacks and whites have to approach me for me while Hispanics have to think of me as commanding? NO. It means that people who have certain accomplishment expectations trained in the normal Black and White *standards* (not necessarily blacks or whites themselves) are more likely to look past me in a crowd unless there's something specific they want from me personally. And that's actually how I prefer it. (Don't come to me just because you want something or want to figure something out.) On the other hand, people trained in the Hispanic *standards* of accomplishment (not necessarily Latinx themselves) are slightly more likely to assign me "he's alright" points "but don't go there if you don't have to." And that's also how I prefer it. So it turns out that being low-average height works well for my selective personality. We'll get to race expectations shortly.

What kinds of accomplishment invitations does your height send?

Weight

Unlike height, weight is not about what you're expected to be able to do around others, but about what others condition *themselves* to do around you.

- **Heavy** people leave the expectation that more energy will have to be spent around them. More expression, more performance, et cetera. As former cavepeople, we see heavier people as getting what they want from us more easily in a close encounter (unlike tall people from afar), and we also see them as harder to take down in a fight; bigger people feel more demanding of something. Depending on other traits like the face, this could consist of stressful demands, performance demands, enjoyment demands, or any number of other debits to our energy, but the bigger person announces the requirement for more of it from others. It doesn't mean they are *actually* demanding though. Only that the announcement their body leaves upon strangers *suggests* this to that stranger. And this leads us to an important point:

Why would a soul choose a body that announces something other than what he is? There are all kinds of reasons, but the simplest one is that your body isn't for you only. It's mostly for others. You look the way you look largely in order to attract the kinds of attention you attract. Your soul's mission may be to work alongside the things you attract, but in almost all cases you will also have something that you've dedicated your life to working *against*. Racism. Foolery. Bad art. Whatever. And your body will be designed to attract certain kinds of support AS WELL AS certain kinds of counter-situations against which you are set to work. Some aspects of your body are perfectly designed to attract things that irk you. Other aspects will surely get you in trouble prior to your learning to control them (or yourself) as part of your mission. Stereotype-validation, resting face, and untamed word usage are all things that we may have been trained into, whose re-trained correction is part of our role in the world.

- **Slim** people, cave assumption-style, are seen as needing less of another's energy—and often being more energetic themselves. If bigger people are harder to take down in a fight, slim people are harder to catch for drawing into a fight in the first place. There is also an association with slim people limiting the things they allow around them. So comes the notion of pickiness. In terms of personal conflict, slimmer people are often seen as irritable (internally irritated) while bigger people are seen as dramatic (situationally irritated).
- And people of **normal build** are often seen as <u>socially</u> irritable in conflict. Having a normal build means that there are fewer assumptions made about your energy-level requirements, and again there can be as much advantage in this as there are in other builds. With no assumptions on your energy requirements, people must associate with you based on matched needs rather than how much will be demanded of them (bigger people) or how much they will be unable to meet demands (slimmer people).

If your height gives others an impression of your command power over strangers (accurate or not), your build gives them an impression of how much energy they'll need to (or be able to) spend on you. Both from afar.

What does your build say to strangers?

Skin Color

From a far enough distance, skin color comes in four tones: really light, really dark, not as light, and not as dark. Thanks to the migration patterns of early humans,

- **really light** is associated with broad European and some East Asian traits—communication/formal social structure-focused and intellectual;
- **not as light** is associated with other Asian and some Latin American—tight community and tradition focused;

- **not as dark** is associated with later original groups like India-Indian, some Western and other Asian, and other Latin American—individual-defined-against-community and actively-obligated dynamic focused; and
- **really dark** is associated with still other American, African, and Aboriginal populations—survival action focused.

All over the world (but certainly not everywhere), lighter groups are more likely to be held in higher status than darker groups, and that could be because, very broadly, lighter groups are newer on the evolutionary tree—with all the old societal mechanisms for perpetuating themselves plus newer ones on top of this. It's easier to see dark as more primitive and less tamed. (In terms of these four broad tones, I fall in the really dark category, and can tell you that our society is still very unequal in terms of where its social role inertia points these groups.)

From white to light brown to brown to dark brown, your skin color—until recently in the West—has been an announcement of evolved communication, developed societal tradition, kin and close relations in a work-based class, and basic human behaviors. Nowadays though, it isn't cool to admit to having these stereotypes, and many of us truly don't think of them *except* when we need to make generalizations about societies we don't belong to or haven't been accepted into—about which we know little. Accordingly, even where fewer and fewer people see color in their daily dealings, your skin color remains an announcement to <u>yourself</u> about the announcements you automatically make to others regarding how your type of person thinks social aims should be advanced. Whew. That was a lot. Let's try it again.

Skin color (not race or ethnicity yet) **is your framework for what you think your class of people does to advance social mobility—for your own type or for others.** Skin color is less about you and more about how you see *the expectations placed on you* for social advancement.

- **Lighter groups** like whites in America have less of a reason to think about skin color at all. The advantage here is that social advancement can happen with fewer occasions for hindrance-by-association.
- **Brown groups** have a social framework for advancement built on who is allowed and excluded from their circle, with light browns typically enjoying more advantages than their darker equivalents. The advantage here is that the opportunities for true connectedness among friends and associates—social support—is greater, where lighter groups may be expected to move socially even with little community to back them.
- **Darker brown** groups have a social framework for advancement built on having to form social systems of their own, for the lighter systems that disallow the dark ones' easy mobility. The advantage is that these groups, broadly speaking, are less likely to give a damn when outside standards are imposed on them, increasing socialized resilience.

Suppose you're a soon-to-be soul getting ready to be born in the US. Suppose your views of the broad social opportunities available to the groups you are by default plugged into, <u>do</u> matter to you. Then you might need to pick a skin color non-randomly. Want social opportunities with less of the processual hassle? Being white will help. It's no guarantee that you'll escape *sociological* hassle for it though (privilege shaming). Do you want a solid grounding in community and groups, even if it makes social *status* more difficult? Being brown will help. And if you want a slightly simpler mobility path from here, being lighter brown will aid this. Not a fan of the formalism? Want more of the right to say what you really think without making all kinds of enemies? Or did you come to shake people up? Black or darker brown in a lighter environment will do.

Briefly on Race and Ethnicity

Once a distant person gets close enough to you to observe your features, your race and ethnicity begin to kick in. Race can be thought of as the feature-based analog to skin color. Whereas skin color tells how you think of others thinking about your class, **race tells you how people are trained to actually act around your class broadly.** Although the 6-10 basic (American census and global cluster) racial types do come with certain packages of information in the here US, I won't list what each race tends to imply here because one of the main points of this book is for you to be able to better choose your intimate partners on all levels. It turns out that race can be critically important in shaping the kinds of people from whence you choose your best partners, yet when you get around them you'll find that, thanks to other qualities besides your looks, the race platform ends up being very wrong.

This will seem nerdy but I'll make the analogy anyway. There is a game franchise out there called Smash Brothers for the Nintendo systems. There, characters like Super Mario can battle it out with the pilot Fox McCloud or Princess Zelda. Mario's default game type is that of cute action. Fox's base game is a space shooter. Zelda's often not even fully playable, and she comes from an adventure game. If you consider the games from whence these characters originally come as their "race," then you may think you know something about them, their costars, or whatever. But then they all meet up for some Smash, beating each other's asses in a fighting game which doesn't match anywhere any of them came from. Race works like that. We can think of your race as a kind of wireframe for spelling out people's reactions to your type for as long as you continue to walk among those who care about it. But once you finally settle on people whose reaction to you personally is based mostly on you yourself and not your physical blueprint, race stops being that kind of announcement and starts acting more the way skin color does: one more factor for strangers to judge—whether mainly in your mind or mainly in actuality.

Ethnicity is like race, but with assumptions about social and political history attached. It is **your announcement to strangers telling them how to act when the group with which you are associated does things that affect them in the world.** I find this absolutely fascinating.

While many people (including myself) lament the problems of racism in the world, our race—and even more so our ethnicity—is like a magic portal connecting us to places we've never been. Granted it's often negative if you're an American traveling abroad with that well-meaning arrogant confidence of yours, but still...the idea that I can be treated differently because someone who looks like me is doing something strange elsewhere in the world is really neat, I think. Your ethnicity is a kind of commitment to connect to and accept the treatment of a group that leaves similar impressions as you, scattered all over the world. If you never had a mind to fight or journey alongside anyone besides yourself in the bigger social world, other people who share your skin color, your, nationality, your sex, or your features may compel you to feel what they're feeling anyway.

Who does your ethnicity put your next to?

What has your race caused you to experience or not experience in close interactions? And when you've experienced it, what have you done in response to benefit yourself from it? That's what your race in this particular life of yours is for.

My own race has caused me no direct problems, but many indirect problems, and has made me aware of many closed opportunities in broader society and in relationships. Addressing the doors closed to people for no other reason besides who they remind strangers of, is a large part of what drives all of my work, including books like this one (on self-acceptance and understanding in relationships). Thanks largely to my experience as a black male with an uncommon name, my life's purpose is to open doors that other people closed on me because they couldn't be bothered to know me. It's an example of how race is useful for triggering certain issues while you're surveying the social landscape, but in the end acts as more of a means to your setting good standards for your exchanges with other interactants.

Your Sex

Are you male or female? In the modern US, it doesn't matter so much from a distance or up close. But in partnerships, oh how it matters a lot! I talk about this in depth in my previous book *Black Male Feminism*, and the short version is that, given a foreign situation, **biological males are trained and expected to go out there first, gather data later**. Independent, interruptive action is the standard. Meanwhile, **biological females are trained and expected to gather data first in a foreign situation, then take care of business** once the situation is sufficiently known.

As a rule of thumb (though certainly not gospel), the leadership research suggests that we prefer male leaders when uncertainty reigns, while we prefer female leaders in systems that are firmly known and established. At the time I am writing this book, I work at a college as the Data Analyst among a group of 11 managers, and am the only male. The women I work with truly kick ass as bosses and are some of the best, strongest, and most decisive people I've ever worked with. The thing about a room full of female managers that differs from a group of male managers (which I've also experienced previously) is that the former people are more collective, more attentive to others outside the room, and generally less apt to argue needlessly when there's work to be done. This isn't to say that female bosses are better than males, but it is to say that the dynamic for gathering information first, *then* making conclusions has been something I've seen. If the college were in a more uncertain position and required more man-bullets, who knows? But even among tough bosses, the way the male-female difference plays out seems to support a couple of general conclusions from anthropology.

- **Males** are trained to compete with each other for outgroup cooperation.
- **Females** are trained to cooperate with each other amidst outgroup competition.

No this doesn't mean all men fight and all females cooperate. It means that if you're a soul and you really want to be socially trained to assert against the unknown, you'll benefit from being male. If you want to be trained to socially assert in the known, given that you're trained to first make the unknown known, then you'll benefit from being female. **Your sex is how you were <u>trained</u> in the process of (and conditions for) asserting your will.**

Your sex is how you were societally <u>trained</u>. Not necessarily what you *accepted* as training (sexual identity). Not necessarily with implications for the kinds of partner you prefer (gender). It's just training, and outlines how strangers continue to make assertion-related expectations of you throughout life.

Dress

The good news about all of the above is that you can take whatever announcements your body makes to the world and modify them fairly simply by how you dress. Are you a rich person who doesn't want to be bothered by others about that fact? Put on a middle classer's clothes. Are you a male who's not necessarily diggin' the macho pressures? Dress in less macho clothes. Do you have a problem getting the people you want to notice you? Dress noticeably. Combined with all of the surface body characteristics above, if there's anything you'd like to modify (at least a little) in terms of how strangers see you, you can influence it with dress. You can dress in line with a particular culture, a particular attitude, or a particular bearing. Just as the food you eat becomes a part of you, the dress you adopt can become a part of your effect on others too.

The Face, The Voice and The Mannerisms

The kinds of expressions that a person can display are too numerous to list, but just like the dimensions we've used, they tell that person's story regarding her approach to Self, Other, and World. The face, besides projecting numerous indicators of a person's health, habits, and history, most commonly serves as a window to the person's attitude. In particular, your resting face gives others a tool for understanding your attitude towards what they might offer. It tells them whether you really want to be where you are, or if you'd rather be doing something else—if you're too focused to be bothered, or minding your own business. That is, your face tells others what your attention (and by extension, *intention*) invites to you. People will be attracted or repulsed by the idea of approaching you for certain things accordingly.

An associate of mine, Sherron is a Master Chinese Face Reader, and she has a talent for telling you all kinds of things about your health and history that you yourself might have even forgotten. Your face is such a rich source of information that it would take a whole book to describe this feature alone. To keep it simple we'll just say that **your face acts as a kind of filter for certain kinds of experiences coming to you easily**.

- Take a moment to look at your face in the mirror.
- As you look in the mirror, consider what kinds of people have an easy time approaching you just to get to know you.
- Now think about what kinds of partners or general company *those* people tend to attract.

If you never knew what your face said to others before this, you may be surprised. (I was.) The end result goes like this:

> My face attracts people who seem to pick [this type] _____ as close friends and partners. Those people tend to have _____ as a main feature of their personality.

Now suppose you completed the above sentence and the result wasn't that positive. Or maybe the results were positive, only to change when you take the makeup off or exit dating mode. What if your face attracts something that typically ends badly, because the people who came to you thought they were getting something else? What do you do? Most of us can't just try something else like Lon Chaney.

Face Rewind

So there's good news, bad news, and interesting news about your face. The good news is that a general change in your outlook (and thus your default expression) may be all it takes to attract different people. You probably suspected that much. The bad news is that, if you're expressive enough in the face you show to the world (no poker plays), you may be one of those people who attracts the same kind of person again and again even if it typically ends up being a fail. But watch this. Just like your ethnicity, there's something magical in the face which is as close to karmic as many of us will get: attracting the same kind of person is your way of hitting rewind on a dynamic built into your psychology. Like being able to live a second life within this single one, a replayed signal to another which leads to a replayed script with the new person also gives you an opportunity to reconsider all of the asshole things you did to that last person, or the messed-up things you positioned them to do to you. No matter how bad the other person may have been, if you catch yourself in a rerun like this, the ball is in your court not theirs. This is your opportunity to fix one of your dimensions which may be in need of repair.

Your face is one of the central Other-triggers you use to invite second chances to yourself for retrying the kinds of situations attracted by your outlook. So it's not a bad thing that you keep attracting that undesirable type. It's your opportunity take a psychological stand amidst whatever that situation involves. Once you've made the stand, you can look forward to never seeing that pattern play out in the same way again.

Mannerisms

Your mannerisms: how you talk with your hands, cover your face, mess with your hair... What are they for? Mannerisms are your way of *telling other people* what your body is interested in doing *without you telling yourself*. They represent the tells which call others' attention to things you're doing, and invite them to form extra opinions about you that you don't even know about. The guardians tell me that mannerisms, especially the ones you display subconsciously, are "potentializing." That is, if pronounced enough, they have the ability to hijack people's story about you once you're absent. So they are what gets traded out from the potential world to replace parts of what you tried to convey as real company. Some mannerisms are overt while others consist of things you *don't* do. Some mannerisms (like picking your nose and looking at it) are typically considered bad while others (like neglecting to make eye contact) will vary in goodness and badness depending on the culture of the observer. So we can't list them here. What we will note is that sudden reversals in how people deal with you, given no obvious motivation, may be related to something they've read in "potential-you"—partly through your mannerisms. Also note that your style of texting and phone conversation can contribute to this too. **Your mannerisms suggest how "absent-you" should be viewed in the World**.

Voice

There is the voice and there is the speech pattern. These give others hints of your intelligence, temperament, what motivates you, and what kinds of thought patterns you will apply when others join your world. Here we have a display of your Self's toolkit for understanding what it encounters, thus making the voice a valuable indicator of whether you and the other person will be able to see eye to eye on topics you encounter together, and how you respond to those topics. With a special emphasis on your idiolect (your personal dictionary of go-to words), your voice and speech show others the realms in which your perspective differs from everyone else's. **Accordingly, it is also useful for telling others what they should truly come to you for to have conveyed to them**.

The above may seem obvious, but the guardians tell me that the voice is the primary "resonator" for an individual. Every time it is used, it marries a person to a large basket of ideas, frequencies, connotations, and so on. We can consider our voices to be a system of shopping carts continually being shipped out full of stuff from our mental store. Positive words, short words, academic words, words with a lot of "ah's" for passing a mouthful of breath or a lot of "ee's" fit for more smiling and wincing—the sounds we make with the voice will serve to trap others in our mental jail or take those others on a liberating journey every time we issue them forth. So **our words create spaces for us to put others in; when piled-on, those same words eventually confine those others to a certain select group of preferred responses to us**. If you use a lot of business words you will put the other person inside of a psychological business. If you talk a lot about faith you will put some people in a church, other people outside of one— figuratively that is, but you get the idea.

Improve Your Words

We don't often pay attention to the words we use because it really can be a lot of trouble to change such a long-standing habit as language use. But I've found that one of the best ways to start improving the effect of your words on others is to find things that interest you in the regular course of improving yourself, and use words that you like from those situations. Meanwhile, you can drop words that raise ideas which annoy you. Once I started teaching political science, I really started liking the word "policy" and disliking the word "politics," because in my mental shopping mall the former implies solutions that people worked at and the latter implies rancor. Another one of my favorite words is "interesting." As a scholar I use it liberally as a way of saying "thanks for giving me something to think about besides the normal bullshit out there."

Someone once told me that words are a billboard held momentarily before other's perception. The more you use words that you like, the more you'll attract things that prefer to dwell in that room you've created. On the other hand, the more you use words or names you hate or those which cause you to load angry things, the angrier you'll be and the more you'll attract things that love to live in angry spaces. For people who have been ugly to me or people whom I've come to disrespect, I typically refer to them as "the coworker" or "the third stepmother," or something like that. But I won't use their name, even to myself. I've found that conjuring the specific person doesn't do me any good in the sanctity of otherwise pleasant communications (either with myself or with friends); there's no need to invite unnecessary craziness into my mental home. This, by the way is one of the single most useful things I've ever done to create lasting happiness in my life:

A trick for you

As soon as you realize that the very use of a word or a name fills you with stress or anger—especially if that feeling seems to spread instantly to anyone you talk to about it—start trading out that word for a reference to a generic role instead.

Not "Mary." Not "my-ex." It's more like "the girl from school." I'm telling you, this is powerful. Spare yourself the rage. Spare your friends.

The voice and speech not only expose your thought patterns to others, but create spaces full of attached ideas in which those others (and you) must temporarily dwell. That's why unsolicited criticism, words that brush another off, and non-uplifting social opinion can really whittle away at an initially expressive relationship. You can only box someone in so many times before they begin to see *you* as an obstacle.

That's it for the public stuff. And now for the rest of the body.

Less Popular Body Parts

Since the central focus of this book is on sex and the intimacy, we'll limit our discussion of the rest of the body to the standard areas of interest: the chest, stomach, hips, and thighs. Before we do that, however, I'd like to note a general rule for viewing other body features such as the forearms, hands, neck, and feet.

As a rule, bodies are compared against other bodies in the eye of the viewer. What is considered normal in one population of viewers may be considered extreme in another, and the extent to which a particular body region is seen as extreme on either end of the proportion scale or extreme on either end of the common-uncommon scale will depend on who you're being compared to. That said, body regions that get frequent comments can be thought of as attention attractors for those commenters, highlighting whatever evolutionary function the body region plays. Longer necks strike us as curious while shorter necks strike us restricted—both in terms of how the person (and we ourselves) can see things. Gaunt hands seem more technical while plump hands seem more broadly open—both in terms of the precision with which the user operates things. Whatever the body region, our reason for paying attention to it on ourselves combined with its noteworthiness in another makes the relevant quality noteworthy in the other. Of course, it's the average reason for paying attention to it across all people which gives the area it's meaning—not just the quirks of the few people who look at you specifically.

Suppose then that you have muscular biceps. We tend to pay attention to our biceps as a shallow measure of strength, age, and (for some) the kind of discipline associated with a more holistic exercise routine. Muscular biceps will partly announce to others a certain level of vitality that you possess overall, and will be meaningful to people who value this. The same holds true for any region we can name.

Taken as a whole, **the less popular parts of the body tell others more about how we apply our efforts to certain tasks**. Hands for handling and manipulating, forearms for blocking, calves for running and elevating yourself higher on toes, shoulders for resting protective coverings on, and feet for holding up the self during traversal. The feet in particular have an association with Pisces and the spirit in astrology, as these are what leave a literal impression of where you've been. Noteworthy **feet announce a noteworthy means of leaving your impression on a place**.

The Chest

In both men and women, the chest is where our heart is. Things close to us that we nurture, and the expectations that others have for our ability to nurture are indicated here. The lungs and our airy sustainment also live here, so there's also an association with how much social sustainment and fuel from the air around us we'll need. As was the case with the whole body, the chest and other regions can have two basic size dimensions, plus another one for unusualness. **In men, the size of the chest is an announcement of <u>protective</u> strength for potential partners** while **the tone of the chest is more of an indication of <u>attack</u> strength**. And this should make sense if you think about what it takes to throw a lot of punches. Both of these are connected to what would be done on behalf of the partner, against other men. The nipples are not as important here as they will be on women, but as will be the case with women, men's **nipples show the size of the window of opportunity through which that nurturing action can be accessed**. A man with a big, cut chest and small nipples may be able to beat another man's ass in a fight for his mate, but getting him to *care* enough to fight for his mate may be another matter.

There's clearly a vast difference between how much we expect women to nurture compared to men. In women, the breasts can be various shapes and sizes, with **volume roughly announcing the capacity to nurture, sagging indicating the ability for the nature of that nurturing to change spiritwards (downwards) over time, asymmetry indicating differences in how she nurtures in a giver versus receiver role,** and **pointedness indicating the ability of that nurturing to be specifically directed versus broadly supplied**. None of this indicates whether the woman (or man in some cases) will *actually* be nurturing, only what a viewer can <u>expect</u> and react to while observing. The nipples, as in men, indicate the size of the "access point" for drawing that nurturing out of the breasts, and the **areolae for breastfeeding promote the observer's memory or strong impression of what that access was like**. In the less common case of puffy nipples in both men and women, the memory is more likely to promote itself rather than needing to be actively recalled. But most of this is obvious when you actually think about memorable chests, is it not?

The Stomach

The stomach is where we process the nurturance we've taken in. The chest nurtures others. The stomach channels the nurturance received from others to where it is needed. As usual, a person's stomach has two form measures plus a third for its more unique features. A **big stomach suggests a big appetite for nurturance** of any kind, including information, company, tangible items, love, busyness, or anything else. Notice, however, that I've left out food.

Frequently in the chapters after this one we'll need to rely on a view of ourselves as structured packages of energy. You know, molecules and such. Thinking of the food we eat as energy, we stop looking at it simply as an object to be stuffed into our mouths and more as a patterned collection of vitamins, acids, dyes, plants, and animal products which get merged into ourselves. More food means more packages of patterned energy for whatever your body plans to do with it. Don't think of food as food. Think of it as patterned energy.

A big stomach announces a bigger processing station for the energy a person nurtures themselves on. Often this means a greater tolerance for stress and drama. Sometimes this means a great capacity to store other's hope for the future. Which one it is and whether the big stomach is natural to the bearer will be related to whether he or she uses what is stored to help others or damage themselves. At the other end, a **small stomach indicates a smaller storehouse for processing nurturance**. Sometimes this indicates an intolerance for all but the most specific inputs, other times it indicates a rigorous filter for what one engages. Which one it is and whether the small stomach is natural to the bearer will be related to whether he or she denies certain nourishment because they have been damaged or because they are disciplined.

Stomach tone indicates regular attention to maintaining one's processing station for nurturance.

Hips and Waist

As with the chest, there is a vast difference between the male and female pelvis in terms of what the forms mean, though the two definitely serve a related function. **Wide hips on a woman announce the capacity to care for what she creates** (rather than herself as above), while **a shapely or toned behind indicates both a man and woman's capacity for travel and exploring new places**. It's the reason we humans evolved butts in the first place: for walking upright long distances. At this point on the *Sapiens* timeline a bigger butt won't help you walk better, but it will get you noticed as you walk—especially if you're a woman. So while the hip size announces creation-nurturing and childcare in an observer, butt size announces having your public traversals be easily visible among potential viewers. This is a measure of the public image in both men and women, but to the extent that women are more likely to have this quality pronounced and socially trained to be observed by men than the other way around, the quality is more celebrated in women than it is in men. For men, the chest and biceps are better indicators of the public image in societies where men aren't as heavily judged by their creation-nurturing, but by their strength and power over other men.

The Sex Organs

The **vagina and penis are a woman and man's bridges for co-creating most fully with each other**. The former acts something like a doorway for the other while the latter acts more like an entrant. Extending this analogy a bit more, **the shape and features of the vagina are a measure of how much peripheral complexity is available to the partner when attempting to issue power towards her one on one**, while **protrusions like a dangling clitoris and a full mound show the partner how much she can be expected to challenge them or cushion against them** respectively. Where some vaginas are ornate with folds and differentiated textures, others are a simple slit. These announce to the viewer the amount of reason needed to "watch where one is going" in the use of power with the woman. The simpler the door, the greater the need for observation. The more complicated the door, the more any reasons for observation will be made clear up front.

"Watching where one is going" by the way is a phrase I heard from the guardians while writing this. I asked what was meant by that last paragraph and they said "during intercourse with someone you don't know well, you are effectively an intruder." Apparently ornate pussies are extraverted, simple ones are introverted regardless of the character of their owners, and as with any unique feature, command different levels of attention. But an intruder upon an innocuous house may open himself up to lot more than he bargained for if he thinks the surface invite is all there is. There was some indication here that there was the potential for more surprises for the partner in the power response of one type of vagina owner than another. Many of these surprises were reserved for later events of various kinds outside of the bedroom. How's that for vague? But that's what I got. Apparently the vagina and the penis are up there with the face and the voice when it comes to diversity of effects in the eyes of the average interactant. At least when you're co-creating.

The **penis is the man's tool for influencing and exercising power against the partner one on one.** Penis **length is an announcement of how much the owner can make his influence felt in a one on one power exchange.** Penis **girth is an indicator of how effective that influence is in compelling the interactants' response**, regardless of whether the influence is deep or shallow. A **hooked penis shows an owner whose sexual and creative development asserted itself actively in a way that the owner had to accommodate**, and is also an indicator of the realm in which the owner asserts that creation. Heavier contact with the left leg desensitizes the body map on the brain's right side. Heavier contact on the right leg desensitizes it on the left side, making it easier for the owner to be stimulated on the side to which the penis leans. A downward turned penis is better equipped for rear entry vaginal sex than a straight one. An upward turned penis is better for frontal entry than rear, and a straight penis is better for general coital engagement. But as usual, you will do whatever you do in the bed. It's the equivalent forms out of the bed that we'll look at here.

Bold and facing, **an upwards penis designed for frontal sex is one designed for forward engagement with the partner**. The dynamic is face-to-face, feedback for feedback, and is **more interpersonal than psychological**. On the other hand, a **downward penis designed for rear entry is more for sensation-based engagement for the partner, but image-based engagement for the man**. In other words, when we are facing each other we are Other to Other. When I am facing your back, we are [my World projection] to [your Self feeling]. That is, the one being rear-entered feels the sensation within themselves rather than in direct response to the partner, while the one rear entering has an interactant, but not facing them; so this second person has sex in the style of one engaging the world. When I think about this I am reminded of Snoop Dogg's album Doggystyle (which I grew up on) and how doin' it from the back was the thing. Form-wise, **rear entry allows the entrant to make a statement to the abstract world more than a direct one to his partner**, and in the context of 90s gangsta rap, that makes sense. Although it's only one of many positions, giving special privilege to doggystyle depersonalizes the partner similar to the way Aries fucking does.

At some point in a man's life, he likely encounters two topics. One of big dicks and the other of premature ejaculation. In form speak, **having a "big dick" means meeting a societal threshold for being influential in a one-on-one (Dimension 8) physical power exchange**. But if the aim of this kind of sex is to exercise a kind of power over the partner, there are many ways to do that regardless of perceived bigness. What we announce physically doesn't say much about what we do (or even what partners want) in actuality—with the full array of additional tools, tricks, and psychological tactics at our disposal. **Premature ejaculation** is premature according to some standardized lap time that nobody knows, **where the assumption is that, once the man has peaked, the woman has no further access to pleasure. It is an announcement of how quickly the man will abandon his partner**

for something else. Actually, I have a story about that which may help men who have this alleged "problem." I'll talk about it in Dimension 12.

In any event, maybe you can see how the comparison stuff can really deflate a person for reasons that don't have to be reasons. The pressures for women are different, but analogous. To be hot, to reach multiple orgasms, to have the perfect level of physical comfort with the partner, to even enjoy sex at all—the lore runs deep. As do the sources of shame.

On Shame

Now is a good time to talk about shaming. In general, shaming is easier to accomplish when a group of people are able to perpetuate a standard without being forced to display it. If they did display it or promote the practical effects of it, the shamed person would have a better chance of recovering. This holds even in cases where the shamed person is unable to address the issue to the group's liking: Suppose, for example, I am gay and I live in a community that doesn't like that; the shame culture tells me that my preferences make me nasty and therefore I can't fit in. But they won't expose their own preferences or show me how to fit in despite mine. If we consider shame to be a feeling of diminished motivation to stand behind something you expressed while now wishing you would have expressed it to a certain party's liking; and if we consider guilt to be a feeling of increased disharmony towards oneself in light of something you expressed while now wishing you would have expressed it to a certain party's liking instead, then guilt and shame both rest upon another party's approval and both involve abandoning where you stand. Some people say that guilt is one of the worst sentiments you can feel, because it amounts to hurting yourself in light of others' opinions. Beyond sex, many people face the more general issue of guilt over being who they are instead of who they are not, and that guilt carries over into relationships that exist even outside of the shamer's reach.

In order for guilt or shame to apply to you, you need to 1) wish you did something to someone else's liking and 2) turn away from the way you originally did it, towards some other way. Although there are certainly occasions where we could have been better in hindsight and where both conditions hold, our old selves effectively lack the benefit of our current selves' hindsight. If we really wish to change badly enough we can start now, but our old selves can't just cease to be. People who shame you but won't help you start anew (or those who won't help you fit in with what you currently have) don't deserve to be listened to. They give judgment without solutions, goals without a practical direction fit for *your* life. Can you ever meet the standards of people who won't show you the blueprint for putting those standards in action? It's their standard and they're the ones dissatisfied. Why don't they help *themselves* be pleased with *you*?

Now I know this easier said than done. But where your self-worth is concerned, people who measure you but never bother to know your perspective very often have some other inner discontent that drives them to be bothered by you. Your identity is yours. In the chapters that follow we'll be discussing ways to own that identity, and you'll likely encounter many areas of pleasure that others have never even thought of. It is essential to own everything you have as of now. If you don't like what you see, you can start changing it at any time. What you shouldn't do is adopt "increased disharmony towards yourself" or "diminished motivation to stand behind something you expressed" over having shown something which was the best you knew at the time. Being big, being gay, being kinky, having uncertain mannerisms...being short, being tall, whatever. If you expressed it you expressed it. Tomorrow might be more of the same. Or not. But no one who shames you for yesterday without a plan to help you "fix it" today is worth abandoning yourself for. Pick new validating words, drop unsupportive names, and escape that space. Your body is *your* announcement. Anyone who got to know you would see that. And much more.

The Thighs

Lastly, the thighs are the part of the body which both supports our upper torso and lifts our lower legs. So they have to be strong. Like the hips, the thighs show how much of a lap you have for sitting on and caring for a visitor (even if it's just their eyes). **On a woman, the thighs serve a role from the front similar to that of the butt from the rear, and show where the public image is a matter of discipline, normal effort, or high aims for status.** Such correspond to small, medium, and large thighs accordingly. Also, thighs can be muscular, fit, or not. These show where the owner has a defining public activity as part of their image. **The thighs on a man are a general measure of his presence in the public space—that is, how (un)able he is to hide from attention if he seeks to do so.**

Summary

This concludes our tour of the body. The final point of all this is to get an understanding of yourself as a series of impressions on other people. Even though your body is your own, its effects are intended more for others than for yourself. That doesn't mean, however, that anyone among those others has the right to judge you, shame you, or limit your use of that body in ways that are meaningful to you. If it harms none, so shall it be. By understanding your effects on others as a physical presence, you gain a powerful lens for understanding your effects as a psychological and social one. With that, we're now ready to explore the remaining nine dimensions.

8 DIMENSION 12: *It Starts With a Vibe*

Have you ever met someone who simply oozes sexuality? Someone who brings such an intense air with them that you may be uncomfortable being around them? Some people carry such a heavy kind of passionate interest in the imaginative sides of experience that others are able to feel that passion in turn. This is the entry point to **Dimension 12 sex**, properly called **Sleepwalking**.

Dimension 12 sponsors World-Water sex and creativity. It revolves around Watery feelings and wants, but not those belonging to you or anyone you're interacting with. Instead, World-Water highlights the feelings associated with a situation—the kind we get glimpses of when flirting and during certain kinds of fully public foreplay.

The less touch you have,

the less obvious advances you make (if you make any at all), the less you actively do to reel in the other person

while still building up their pleasantly enjoyed intensity in your company,

the closer you are to Dimension 12. But flirting isn't the only way to pull this off. The main route to this kind of exchange is actually through shared, deeply intertwined imagining.

Dimension 12 is the first type of sex that requires a *de*-emphasis on physical contact. While a lot of us are taught about flirting and foreplay as a pathway to full-blown sex, many of us are actually forced to get good at Dimension 12 simply because the more physical exchanges are too often unavailable to us. Remember the chapter on "I love you?" Here's here we'll begin to put it to use: Since the default way we're taught to handle married or taken people—whom we also like a lot—is often to deny the feeling at all, we may spend decades learning to suppress very genuine feelings towards them. If you and they have the discipline for it, however, you can engage in Dimension 12 with no harmful effects on anyone's formal commitments. The secret to good Dimension 12 sex—eventually physical or never so—is to be okay with feeling something deeply in the company of another without requiring that they prioritize your physical pleasure, without fear that you're betraying someone emotionally, and without the need to force any further escalation of the exchange. Dimension 12 consists of truly going with whatever comes, in mutual pleasure with the other person.

Dimension 12 is one of the trickiest dimensions of the whole group because so much of it requires that you NOT do what we're taught to do in building a relationship, and that you DO do the kinds of things associated with "giving up" on something. That is, more than half of a World-Water exchange involves accepting whatever conditions have already been put on the relationship, as if there is no point in forcing anything. Forcing, escalating, suggesting, throwing hints beyond the ones you and the other naturally throw—none of these will help. They will only force one of you to act, putting you in the Fire dimensions instead. World-Water is also tricky because real success with it almost always requires that you relax your standards for committed relationships. Those rules you have about "not cheating," "never going for that kind of person," "not betraying your normal sweetheart," and "and needing them to show exclusive interest in you too" may need to be set aside in some cases. Not because you plan to break any of those rules, but because the easiest way to kill a vibe is to arrest it for crimes it was never planning to commit. IF you're secure in your own loyalties, IF you can trust yourself, and IF you can really dig what the other person is bringing <u>as it is</u>—without requiring that they change it—you can safely dive in with them without any worries or additional labels for boxing in the relationship. Speaking of labels...

I've entered Dimension 12 with a handful of people over the years, and can honestly tell you that, just in terms of ratios, the Dimension 12 exchanges have been the best, most enduring exchanges of all the types I've had. This should make sense, because when we recall how good or bad even normal sex was—or any interaction for that matter—it is through *memory* that we do it.

There's something about a quality interaction in which everything is simply understood, where you and the other see eye to eye on all that you inspire in each other and none of what you'd burden outsiders with. The desire to do things that spoil the vibe just isn't there. But once you label that relationship—where one day in the middle of a good exchange you suddenly ask for more or mention how you're "just friends" as a way of spelling out boundaries—you often find that things aren't the same thereafter. The magic is gone. Turns out that they were only an Earthy object after all, dressed up in fuzzy feelings. For anyone who's had this happen you know how disappointing it can be. Unless you really do plan to escalate this kind of exchange, do yourself a favor. <u>Don't mess with it</u>. Dimension 12 relationships can truly evolve their own magic if you just let yourself ride them out. Leave the labels and the escalating moves at home. These things get their fuel almost entirely from what goes *unsaid* about the two of you.

Now I know what some people might be thinking. "That all sounds nice, but it doesn't seem as exciting as real sex." But if you believe that, it may be because you've never tried a relationship completely free of imposed requirements. When we think of good sex, we may fall back on the setting, the sensations, and the actions, but the process of thinking itself is also a kind of vibe, know what I mean? Even as I'm writing this, I recall two people who remain dear to me to this day—one married and one separated by rank—where sex wasn't even a remote possibility. But because we connected so strongly through our shared situations, it is much easier to recall them easily with the same kind of deep passion I felt for them back then. The relationship which never needed forms or labels to begin with doesn't need them now. Unlike actions that end, words that get spent, or labeled objects which disappear when the thing itself goes away, the feelings that you felt which were given their radiant character through your time with another need only a similar feeling to restore them as newly as the moment you had them. If you've known people who've given you this, no matter how briefly they were in your life, and if you've freed yourself of the need to wish for more than the perfect satisfaction they've already given you, then you know that a relationship like that can easily eclipse even the best physical sex. If not during the act then at least throughout the years following it. Relationships described by an immersive vibe have a staying power like no other.

And if they change into something more physical, then fine. I'll bet you that most people will still consider the non-sexual time to have been exceedingly valuable though.

The Sleepwalker's Art

Because Dimension 12 is all about the vibe that you and another person reinforce together—dissociated from any Earthy labels, Fiery actions, or Airy communication you might otherwise impose in order to bind it—you may have many other exchange modes involved, but the shared vibe will not be based on any of them. It's the whole situation that counts. So when Dimension 12 takes the form of actual sex, it's often the kind that sends one or both partners to a world outside of themselves. Golden is the sensation, indescribable is the sentiment, with nothing to guide it and nothing to define, only a window for viewing through. Whatever it is you view. While on Dimension 12 most of your focus is on simply continuing your natural movements, similar to the way you drag yourself through every next space just after waking up. And actually, the best way to get good at Dimension 12 is to develop an array of things which you can do with a master's expertise *only* when stone tired. The astrological equivalent of Dimension 12 is Pisces—associated with sleep and dreaming. And that makes the realm of World-Water perfect for "sleepwalkers."

There are two kinds of modes in which we normally see our tired sides bring out the skills in us. One is right before sleep and right before waking. In the land "between actively thinking" and "dead to the world," there are certain kinds of thought that we're really good at having which just don't happen as easily any other way. Whatever that pattern is for you, it is a reflection of your low energy mode which nonetheless continues to diligently produce experiences for you until you finally fall off that twilight line. People who get horny in half-sleep states like this are more likely to love Dimension 12 sex with their partners while people who get worried are less likely to feel secure here. As in waking, you know this is your mode if you feel more creative in states that resemble it. How you act while falling asleep at work can also be considered one of your twilight modes.

Another mode in which we are masterfully active while relatively dissociated is during the making or experience of art. Listening to songs that transport you, dancing, or getting absorbed in an actual creative process will put you in a World-Water state. You're surrounded by a vibe of a particular kind, but your attention is in all places around the object you're engaged with. Now I have some good news and some interesting news regarding this. First, your art mode shows you the kinds of settings which drive your Dimension 12 should you ever wish to go there. The interesting part is that this art mode is THE state you'll be in most of the time after you've spent all your energy. Right before sleep, during a creative process beyond words, at the end of a long stretch of something, and yes, after orgasm. That's right. For you men out there who have been taught to fear "premature" ejaculation and for all you women who consider it to be the end of the night with him, not necessarily. Right after orgasm the man usually doesn't just black out and fall over. Briefly, at least, he enters Dimension 12. Now's the time for him to operate sleepwalker style. If he cares enough about you to just *continue*, you may actually like this version of sex better than the part before. See what happens when it's less about dick, more about fingers, tongues, and...whatever else. Half-dazed (as, for some, half-drunk) is the best time to do all kinds of Dimension 12 things as only a zombie can. Fuck all the social shaming. All the two of you need to do is <u>keep your time together going</u>.

I think it's interesting that the once taboo world of lubricants and pleasure enhancers has now become so common. On the one hand it's good for many people's confidence and enjoyment of sex, but on the other hand it actually drowns out the relational sides of sex at the expense of the physical sensations. As we all know, sex isn't just about sticking things in various holes, but frequently involves people liking each other's company, liking themselves, or even liking the situation itself. But we can't lube a mood. Some of the key parts of the experience really will depend on us. World-Water sex is all about *just continuing*, tired as hell, zoned the fuck out, touching stuff, feeling stuff, making magic with the room you're in. Who knows what your partner's thinking? Who cares? They're zoning out and feeling it with you, without your needing to force anything. And that feels fine.

So you want to enter Dimension 12 with someone? Let's talk about how to do it. If I had to outline some basic steps for this kind of exchange with someone, I'd list the following:

> **Pick a partner who understands or shares your twilight-sleepwalker mode.** How do they act when they're low on energy? Are they cranky while you're chipper? Do they worry

while you simply get comfortable? Partners who don't share (or at least understand) your twilight mode won't work. Still, spotting a good World-Water partner is *very* easy if you know that's what you're looking for. But those partners are almost impossible to recognize if you *don't* know that's what you're looking for. That's because World-Water partners often gain that status due to restrictions preventing them from becoming full-fledged physical partners. So either you or they may disqualify each other for obligated social reasons, even when there's no reason to think you'd cross any real lines.

Pick a partner who shares your creative perspective. There is a very simple test you can perform here, but one you'll need discipline to follow through on afterwards. When you convey something exciting that you've created or brought about, do they seem to share your excitement too? Do they get fueled by the same kinds of creative processes that you do? If only my present self had told my younger self that Dimension 12 would ultimately be my preferred mode, my younger self might have avoided all kinds of pitiful mismatches with my first partners.

So often it will be obvious to you that the person you're with simply won't get as excited about your creations as you will. They may even tear you down or scrutinize your efforts. Maybe the two of you can still fuck. You might even get married eventually. But unless you get on the same page regarding the kinds of emotional *situations* that you each find exciting, Dimension 12 will likely be difficult for you to achieve. What's worse, your ability to create favorable, compatible *memories* with each other independent of the "things" and activities that fill your life will likely be lower. These are the kinds of relationships that work when "stuff" is involved to unite you, but don't work nearly as well when the stuff is removed—where you just have to like each other's energy. The reason we've started the nine remaining dimensions with number 12 is this: In order to have thoroughly satisfying relationships you'll need to be allowed to be happy with yourself too. It's a bummer having a partner who eagerly supports those of your aims which satisfy *them externally*, but won't give the time of day to things that satisfy *you internally*. You know you deserve better than that.

> The third and final piece of advice I'd give (and this applies to every kind of relationship you wish to build to its fullest) is to trust yourself. Give your best towards whatever loyalties you may have, but trust yourself. If he's married but you clearly dig each other, there's no crime in that. If you value the relationship but can't see a convenient way to advance it without messing it up, there's no crime in leaving it alone either. Some relationships need exactly this to be fully realized. It's not necessarily time, but may just be a kind of natural flow. Trust that the fuzzy situation you've put yourself in is okay. For God's sake don't call the thought police or the boundary wardens in on yourself if you don't have to. You're grown. You can respect the obvious cues. Let it breathe.

Conclusion

Because it lives beyond formed limits, a Dimension 12 exchange has the potential to be the best kind you'll ever have, whether or not it becomes sexual. The secret lies in Dimension 12's status as a non-embodied feeling—just like the memory you use to recall anything. Accordingly, this dimension is one of those most resistant to time or changes in circumstance, and can be restored as good as new every time you recall it. There is a catch, however.

Dimension 12 relationships often form because more formal relationships cannot. You'll need to be okay with that. You'll need to be okay with operating on low energy, doing something only in "zone out," staying there for the partner after you've peaked too soon, making something abstract without the normal waking level of focus, and any other analogous state of action in which half of you is somewhere else. If either you or your partner is uncomfortable with this, or if one of you demands something more tangible than this,

Dimension 12 may elude you, and that's too bad. There's a lot to be gained from relationships which are good enough to structure themselves. Ideally all relationships built on a whole greater than our separate parts should have at least some element of this. Even if you're notoriously physical, you might still be served to give World-Water a try. Doing so with a creatively compatible person may change your life.

Remember:

- For a World-Water love that endures, pick a partner who shares the same kind of sleepwalker/twilight/low energy mode and the same foundation for creative enthusiasm as you have.
- Trust yourself. Don't force anything (unless your aim is to put the relationship through a test)
- When you spend time with the other person, JUST CONTINUE! Especially when you've run low on energy...as long as it remains enjoyable. That's the nature of Dimension 12. That man who cums too quickly may transform into a super stud if you let him enter Dimension 12 right afterwards. Embarrassment doesn't have to be the only option. You'll see how this works once you try it.

(FYI: This entire book is being written mostly under dimension 12. I only start chapters when I'm dead tired after work, with zero plans for what's next, and with a good supply of vodka and tea nearby. I often marvel at how my fingers seem to be hitting the keyboard, but I'm not really moving. It's like I'm watching my body type from some other world. That's the Sleepwalker's dimension. Practice it using any songs that put you in an altered zone, and see what kinds of amazing stuff you can do when operating on autopilot.)

9 DIMENSION 9: *Make Me A Star*

It's the kind of sex you brag about. Maybe it was good, maybe it wasn't, but your friends don't have to know that. The way you spin the story, it was absolutely flippin' awesome. This is World-Fire sex. Sex in situations that fulfill people's fantasies and make loud statements to the world. Of course, the fantasies need not be your own and the world does not have to be one that you actually care about.

If you ask a single person to describe their ideal mate, they'll likely give you the basics. *He's nice looking, put together, tough, and makes her laugh. She's hot, sensitive, smart, and determined. They both do their own thing...* but also do everything the describer wants. And neither has any undesirable qualities.

It's likely that the person's ideal mate looks like some easily referenceable star with great features all over. It's also likely that, however they do it, they automatically bring more security of some kind to the describer's world. We can dream, can't we?

The only thing is, we ourselves are imperfect. We're so imperfect, in fact, that it's interesting to describe that same ideal person as usual, list all of our own personality quirks, then add this "perfect person's" hypothetical response to our description of them. Let us see how their perfection stands up then. MWAAAHAHAHAHAHA!

I've known several women, for example who wanted their perfect man to be tough, but also wanted him to kowtow before her every criticism. But then again, she wanted him to "take no shit" from anybody. Except her. But not be a wimp about it when he did it. But not frustrate her demands by disagreeing with her either. What kind of man is this, you ask? A damned basket case. At least he looks good, though.

So you know that you can be a selfish, arrogant, non-listening, complaining, shallow jerk to your partner sometimes. As for that ideal mate you described, how would they handle your selfishness? What would they do when they happily told you they finally closed on that that 7th mansion, and your response was a dissecting criticism? How should they act when, in your toughness, you never give one inch in an argument but will continue kicking the poor fool long after they've dropped to the ground? Bringing it up again and again, whatever it was. What would you do if they faced hardship and weren't as beautiful or easy to get along with as when you first met? Could you stick with them as an ideal if they stopped being hot, rich, or entertaining? Would you say the same thing if it were the other way around? Pretending for a second that you haven't thought about these things, let's just assume that your ideal person followed the only rules you know: your own. Even with all of the perfect traits you might have listed, how would you see them if they handled the situations you presented them in the way that you handle those same situations given to you by others?

That's why we don't have angels as partners. Instead, the people we get are usually perfect for the kind of people *we* are. Except in cases of abuse and exploitation, we attract mates who fit us in several dimensions, not just the dating scene. Our partners match our communication patterns, our distancing behaviors, our physical announcements, our preferred vibes, attitudes, and power styles. More than being just pretty faces, our partners serve as companions to us, sometimes as fellow bill-payers, typically as sources of public validation. For every reason we may have sought a significant other in the first place, we earn a quality in them—or despite them—which addresses that reason. Thus we may not get who we'd wish for, but we will get who we need. It's up to us to separate our negative reasons for partnership (like insecurity, loneliness, and other-pleasing) from our positive ones (like sharing experiences, following a life path, or building something worthwhile). Barring this separation, we'll end up getting someone who teaches us mainly those lessons which explain our current discontentment at the moment. Expect at least a couple of those lessons to be hard ones.

Having a vision of the ideal mate is fine, but there are ways to tweak that vision to better support experiences you actually care to have. For a long time I had a preference for fiery Latinas. Looking back at the Body Parts chapter, I now realize that this was more a reflection of a desire to have my work accepted in my native San Antonio than anything else. Let's call this other-pleasing. As soon as I realized that the fiery Latina also brought problems for me which were related to my views of social mobility in the city, my background frustration with the city at the time began to show up as background frustration in these kinds of relationships. The reason this happens is because even though cities, workplaces, TV channels, and inanimate objects aren't people, we bring our person-centric framework to bear when interacting with them. In the same way that a concept we can't see like God can be dealt with as though human, so too can concepts such as the job market take on enough of a response pattern (against our efforts) as to parallel the people who relate to us in the same way. You will have an easy time seeing French people in the same way you see

France. If France is all about liberty, equality, and fraternity which thumbs its nose at your personal entitlement, you will have an easier time seeing people who thumb their nose at your entitlement in the same way you see France. You might see your job in the same way as you see all obligated work for a paycheck. Or if your attitude is positive, you may see it the way you see all spaces formally designed to draw out your particular skills.

How we see classes of constructs reveals how we see the dynamics they imply as we interact with them. The types of people who provide those same dynamics will be seen by us in a related way.

Getting back to the idea of seeking mates about whom we can brag, our goal then shifts from framing a perfect-looking mate to framing a perfectly complementary one. On top of all of their perfect qualities, we'll want to frame certain things that they lack. Like the thing they were looking for which drew them to "imperfect" us in the first place. Of course we're wonderful, but what is it that we would provide this perfect person that they couldn't get for themselves? Please say it isn't your money or your status.

The point of all this isn't to burst your bubble. You really can attract the kind of perfect mate worth bragging about. If you're already attached and both of you are willing to work at it, you really can build the kind of relationship worth bragging about with your current person. All we're after is a complete picture of what that entails. Not a partial one. It's actually good news that even our most bragworthy relationship will be with a fellow imperfect human. That means the need to be chronically dissatisfied with your current choices goes away. There's no need to wish your ideal were hotter if your handling of their hot popularity would only burden you with relationship maintenance problems. There's no need to wish your ideal mate were richer if their riches would only cover up real failures in your interpersonal emotional space.

This is a situation where it's easier to see other people's obstacles than it is for us to see our own:

Imagine that friend of yours who's always looking for the perfect partner, but whose own faults get magically swept aside whenever he does. Note how easy it is for you to think of all the ways in which he might make the dream partner miserable if he found them. Note how easy it is to think of all of the ways in which the dream partner would have to be pathologically broken in order to even put up with some of your friend's stuff. And if your friend is not above cheating, lying, or stealing from another, scolding, shaming, or selfishly seeking vengeance...Note how easy it is for you to think of all the not-so-friendly ways in which the ideal partner might have to cope. There it is easy to see: the greater these faults in your friend, the less of a complete person their so-called "ideal" partner would actually have to be. Unless that partner simply loved your friend for who he was. Then your friend would have to love himself in order to avoid sabotaging the whole thing, wouldn't he?

We think of ideal mates as satisfying a certain family of conditions (great ones), but there are actually three families of conditions involved:

- the great qualities they have,
- the qualities they would *have to have* <u>in order to stay with us,</u> and
- the qualities which *drive them to seek things that we can help them find* better than most (the not-so-great missing parts of them that chose them to pick us).

These are the World, Other, and Self sides of our bragworthy mates respectively; taken together they can quickly transform that perfect ideal into the person or people you already have available to you. Your mate doesn't just reflect you, they also reflect your vibe, your thought patterns, and your situation in life. They don't typically reflect qualities that you're not equipped to handle, habits you're not able to keep up, or lifestyle patterns you're not poised to meaningfully relate to. So the normal mate turns out to be more ideal than the ideal is, mainly because our ideal is often only a fraction of the real picture that suits us. This is as true for jobs and living situations as it is for people. Your ideal is only possible in the realms in which you frame them and act towards being able to handle them. But in the countless other realms in which you *do not* frame them—the realms of dealing with you, handling their own faults, and sharing creative direction with you, for example—the qualities they possess may look to you like a dice roll on your own lifestyle. With that as a basis, we are now ready to talk about Dimension 9 sex.

An Introduction to Dimension 9

Dimension 9 relationships, the World-Fire kind, **are all about the kinds of things we wish to broadcast to the world at large**. One of the first lessons I learned with this kind of relationship is that not everyone actually wishes to "brag" in the bragworthy dimension. We've spent quite a while talking about the so-called perfect ideal because, in reality, it often doesn't apply to us beyond superficial socialization. The publicly trained ideal assumes that you want in a private partner those things that public populations value. But not everyone brags by bragging. To the extent that bragging is just one way of publicly broadcasting a thing that one is proud to broadcast, bragging is really just one kind of public impression management. It reflects the culture of behavior you are glad to surround yourself with, and in the sub-realm of your sexual relationships it reflects the spaces in which you were proud to be close to another. Generally speaking, you won't attract a satisfyingly broadcastable romantic relationship until you have found yourself a satisfyingly broadcastable "intimacy-culture." Let's define the term right now so we can use it. Dimension 9 will require this.

Intimacy culture is the set of personal and attitude practices that you believe build outstanding intimate relationships, where intimacy is something like the level of close contact you have to others' deeply protected qualities. "Protected" means those aspects of themselves most resistant to being changed from the outside, and which the person insulates from exposure to the average interactant.

Take a moment to think about those situations where you so thoroughly admire the kinds of relationship people built that you wanted that kind of relationship yourself. It won't always be romantic. My favorite relationship is the kind I see in my all-time favorite movie *Lawrence of Arabia*. A dramatic crusade, a visitor open to a culture entirely different from his trained one, a group of determined people in a foreign land fighting for what they believe in with a fierce and undying loyalty...despite how the popular standard may view them as a group. It's romantic I think, but not in the popular dating way. But if ever I wanted a publicly broadcastable relationship, this is the kind my subconscious would want me to build. Were I to spend time in relationships where my mate wasn't a crusader, didn't co-explore, wasn't reliably on my side, but was xenophobic for example, Dimension 9 would elude me. But Dimension 9 is also the realm where one finds satisfaction with the image they broadcast, so it if eludes you then that says something about how you think you've made an impression in the world. What a pickle. Maybe you're not looking to brag everywhere, but at least you'd like to be satisfied with the means through which you project your instinctual passions to strangers. What kinds of passion projection do you admire?

Do you wish to be a crusader, a lover, or a caretaker? How about a fun friend, a deep thinker, or a responsible rock to others? A success, an indomitable power, an artist, a brave traveler, or just a good companion? Or maybe you love watching free spirits roam. Whatever your projected passion, if you were to share that life with another, what kinds of qualities might the person need in order to support you on that path? What kind of personality would make you a star?

When we're not happy (or are unfamiliar) with the lot we've drawn, our passion projection invites stressful motivation. When we *are* happy the motivation tends to be positive. In one case we evolve against the partner, in the other we evolve alongside them. But we evolve either way. A lot of the frustration in our relationships is that we're taught to value fun friends and lovers as ideal mates, but even when this matches us, our social surroundings have all kinds of impractical advice to give about how this should be done. If you're someone who would deep down do better as a good companion however, the ideal may manifest a lot differently from what you were trained to expect. Maybe the Other isn't Prince Charming, but charmingly burdened. Maybe he's not a prince, but needs your companionship as he strives to become one. In this example his need for you may subtract from his perfect qualities, but in some cases this might be better don't you think? What he lacks in his own desirable perfection he donates towards yours.

When we're happy with our lives it's easier to see this. When we're unhappy it's harder.

Every passion projection style has at least three modes for drawing it out: Stressful Other, Harmonious Other, and non-Other. A free spirit projection style may invite partners who cage her in, partners who run free with her or—in the case of a person whose array of ideal traits aren't met by other variables in her circumstances—the absence of a partner entirely. There, she may get a job that compels her free roaming instead. That way she can roam herself right over to a package of expressive outlets that better suits her, partnered or not. As a crusader-traveler type I often attract rebels or conformity-forcers, flakes or nomads, and in between these I'll be the elusive one myself as I go from job to job. Which combinations of qualities are better for me? It depends on what I'm learning at the time. So it is for you. Here are some passion projection styles you might choose from, along with the kinds of people you may attract to bring these styles out of you:

Public Passion Style	Harmonious Driver	Stressful Driver
Fire		
Friend	Ingroup expresser	Outgroup loyalist
Free Spirit	Inspirer-Empowerer	Jailer-Diminisher
Traveler	Learner of the new	Fixer of old upon new, Imposer

		of Excessive New upon Old
Earth		
Success	Pleasable Contentment Holder	Unpleasable Pusher of Further Striving
Deep Thinker	Listener-Prompter	Distractable-Preoccupant
Reliable Rock	Worthwhile Burden Carrier	Unnecessary Burden Carrier
Air		
Lover	Sharer of Love	Rejecter or Love
Companion	Supporter of your thoughts	Overrider of your thoughts
Crusader	Cause adopter	Uninvolved position holder
Water		
Indomitable Power	Malleable subject	Intractable subject
Caretaker	Open to your care	Resistant to your care
Artist	Abstractifier (one who promotes your imaginings)	De-Confuser (one who says your abstraction is confusing and tries to bring it down to their level)

Watch Their Style of Answer

Now I have a neat trick for you which you may like. If you want to know another person's passion projection style (and thus the route to truly supporting them as image projectors in the world), see which of the Harmonious and Stressful Driver tactics they use on you. The worst relationship I ever got into was with a non-romantic partner who used Rejector of Love and Outgroup Loyalist in response to my Imposer of Excess and Open to Care. More than anything, a person's Driver response to you will tell you how they prefer to frame projections of love, and typically has little to do with you specifically. Their response to you is all about what *they* see. As the Open and Rejector cases illustrate, it is very easy to get many of the styles confused. In truth they all overlap. The only thing I can tell you is that listening to what the person is saying can really help this. It's like being able to read minds. Especially if you listen for which of the above stories the person tells you about people besides yourself, you'll get a sense of what they're looking for in Dimension 9. From there it will be up to you how to approach the signals you send to them and those you wish to receive from them.

Wait, there's more.

Yet Another You

As in the body parts chapter, we have characteristics we want AND characteristics we project. The two are often different. And you don't have to have just one. I'd love a Traveler-Crusader relationship, but am most often an Intractable Subject and Unnecessary Burden Carrier in the relationships that come to me. This is an example of the difference between how people see you and how you wish to be seen. Where that difference is great enough in your mind, you will exit relationship after relationship using tactics you wouldn't have thought the other person saw you as using. I find the idea of reconciling the wanted passion versus seen passion to be an exciting thing though, since it is THIS work that you do which has one of the most direct effects on the kind of people you can attract for the long term. There's no need to make any drastic changes.

Next time you're tempted to use a stressful driver on a person who comes to you, use the harmonious version instead.

From there, show the person your actual passion style. If you're not interested in them, show yourself the style.

The effect of these steps is to take the gift given to you and receive it harmoniously, and use that gift as fuel for the kind of relationship you want. Just like the perfect ideal. Even if the person initiating this isn't what you expected. Let their acts be the "I love you" that you've been asking life for.

Dimension 9 Sex

World-Fire sex is less about what you did and how you did it, and more about who you can impress in describing where you did it (the situation that is). Whether the story is all about how you smashed it, how endowed the other person was, or how exotic the experience was, Dimension 9 is your approximation of the passion styles that impress you. The collection of people's practices which support your favorite passion styles are what we'll call intimacy cultures. These are the best places for you to find ideally broadcastable partners.

Because your intimacy culture is a culture and not a single body, it will often incorporate at least one of the Air styles or one of the Water styles. It may also be full of one of the Earth styles of people who encourage one of the Fire styles of action in you and in each other. From your intimacy culture you learn the tactics for successful relating, and integrate those tactics into your outlook for relationships. The good (and perhaps overwhelming) news is that, if you just do the math assuming one of each element alone, you'll see there at least 3^4 or 81 styles of passion cultures out there, and if you assume nothing besides the choice combinations from 12 types there will be 2^{12} (4096) choices. Some of these choices may show up as nationalities, others as lifestyle groups, while others still may draw from communities of practice, so the possibilities are endless in a mere mortal's lifetime.

This is where it pays to be open. Some of your ideally broadcasted sex will be sponsored by the partner, the rest will be sponsored by you and the context you'll ultimately use for describing the event thereafter. The more aversion you show to whole classes of culture, the more you exponentially limit not only your Dimension 9 relationship options, but also your broader Dimension 9 image projection. So even if you're the most materially successful person in the world, your closure to certain cultures will lock you out of the favor that can be shown you by those cultures. Your company and its clients may praise you, but the broader social history written by all people everywhere will still put your name below those individuals who were more universally open than you. In terms of broadcastable exchanges, you'll need to be at least open enough to receive the groups which support the experience you're looking for.

So Dimension 9 sex starts with a kind of cultural identity. Collections of practices which produce those relationship situations you admire enough to enthusiastically train in yourself. Guess where one of the best places to discover yours is? Your college major. This is the collection of people you will have surrounded yourself with after the restrictions of K-12 are no longer there to bind you. How your peers think about the world, and how they train to reconcile their roles in that world are both gateways to the projective surroundings you demand. For those of us who never went to college or whose college experiences were uninformative, your political affiliation and any charitable causes with which you identify will also show this broadly. No it doesn't mean you'll be into animals just because you give to the ASPCA. It does mean that giving hope to the abandoned may be a part of your thing and, by extension, sex in a comparatively abandoned place (or its opposite) may appeal to you as broadcast-worthy. If that's how you frame it, for example. As with World-Water sleepwalking, our bodies follow a blueprint for certain kinds of energy spending. With Dimension 12 it involved action on low energy. **With Dimension 9 it involves the first actions you would prioritize in the world beyond yourself as soon as your obligated exchanges no longer weighed you down**. Hence the connection to voluntary passion broadcast, self-enhancing training, and liberated charity.

You might think that we've gone through a lot of trouble so far, and we haven't even gotten to the sex part. That's because Dimension 9 sex is hard to have consistently. The more you do it, the less of a first impresser it becomes and the more of an expected habit it becomes. "I did it on top of a moving train; in the back of a rollercoaster; in the bathroom of the USS Lexington with a live screencast capturing every butt slap." And which of these is most impressive? To me it's the moving train, but in general the more you list the more those list items melt into a broad wildness. So if that won't continuously impress your image upon the world, how about stories of your own experiences? "When I came I saw the cosmos. I saw Jesus himself. I saw Jesus breakdancin' with some aliens on top of the cosmos. It was like the last boss of Bayonetta 1." Impressive, granted. But not something the world beyond you can easily feel the way you can. And so we fall back on *the* most reliable means of constantly projecting our impressive image onto everyone else in abstract: Our partner's awesome qualities.

Once you have your intimacy culture down, you'll want a partner whose physical qualities embody that culture. If you admire foreign lands, a foreigner to your own background may be helpful. If you admire energetically rich companionship, a bigger build may be helpful. We're talking physical qualities here that strangers in the broad world can observe with their two eyes or at least their ability to imagine. Something the partner displays, has control of, or affects in the world should excite people when we unleash the tale on them. If you want your Dimension 9 ideals to render you a star every time, here's the place where size or scope will definitely matter.

I won't go into the various areas of impressiveness that you may require in your partner. Instead I'll briefly mention how you might learn to tell the story of that impressiveness. Recall that the stock ideal may be much farther away from your active reality than your society suggests it should be. A better route (at least in this dimension) is to get real about the qualities that mate should have which complement *the actual you*, get real about the passion styles you value most, then match up a select quality in the mate which embodies the passion style you've chosen. We actually go through this process all the time when we brag to others about qualities our partners have which we think are shareworthy. *My man's hung like a beast. My wife's fuckin' hot.* These are cases where the partner serves as the thing we broadcast in order to project ourselves in the abstract. Your body is partly for other's remember? Remember that social utility they owe you? Here's where you phone it in.

No matter how plain they may think themselves, everyone has a physical or physically accessible stand-out package which will capture people's attention above and beyond the packages of others. There are reasons why a person would turn away from that hot model and look solely at you instead, and those reasons don't need to involve making fun of you. Instead, that package of impressions we talked about in the body parts chapter constitutes a combined perceivable frequency that nobody else has. Some of it will be easily visible. Some of it will be easily envisionable. Good Dimension 9 sex relies on two things: the intimacy culture you train under and the easily viewable traits of the partner which capture your passion style. Surprise! It's not about sex, but the sex story. In the non-sexual world it's about the story of newly liberated creative potential. If you want good Dimension 9 sex, you'll do almost all of your work in the choice of stand-out partner qualities, intimacy culture tactics, and in the intentional selection of audiences for hearing your gripping rhimes. (*Guitar strum*)

In one sentence, my advice for Dimension 9 is as follows:

> Find a passion culture you like and use its practices and its language to tell impressive stories about your escapades with your partner.

You don't need to tell it in words. Showing it will do. This dimension isn't about how spectacular sex was for you. It's about how spectacularly your story of you and your mate stacks up against the publicly ideal one.

Even if the person doesn't possess traits conducive to Dimension 9, together with you they may yet achieve a worldly status, an effectiveness, or a scope of influence which more than meets your audience's entertainment standard.

10 DIMENSION 5: *Just Playing Around*

Some of the best sex I've ever had wasn't sexual at all, but
took place in creation with other people. Recently, for
example, I had the pleasure of spending a quiet afternoon
with a friend of mine, where we worked on a puzzle together.
We expected several people to show up but no one did. Over
the course of that mostly silent hour though, I experienced a
very real change in feeling. This person, who had been with
me even in times of difficulty, with whom I'd developed a
way of communicating that could endure whether or not
there were words traded—this person to whom I would easily
and automatically push new end pieces as I gathered them
from my own section—gradually became a co-creator not just
of the thing we were working on, but of the environment in
which we worked. I noticed the quiet and semi-cloudy
afternoon, and how there was no one around to slather on
the intellectualism, fill the air with "should"s, or stuff our

space with demonstrations of their own importance. At that moment I was just a guy passing pieces to a girl who was looking for them, both of us headed for the same destination. By the time I realized any of this, my heart rate had already gone up, my breathing had become shallow, and I had already fallen into a state of consuming harmony with this person. And I felt a passion in her presence which settled into a sort of autopilot. I was sleepwalking across the table from someone who was effectively a co-worker, and there was no physical contact that needed to be sought. It was just puzzle building. Yet the feeling was deeper than the one I remember with a more recent sexual partner. The ensuing 30-minute high remained strong until one of us finally checked the time. This was Dimension 12 in feeling, but Dimension 5 in form.

Dimension 5, Other-Fire, *is all about playing around*. It's related to the kind of sex you have for fun, no strings attached. Flings and fuck-buddies and all that. The goal of Dimension 5 is for you to tell someone, "Hey watch this!" And from there you release whatever behavior towards them which you thought worthy of performing.

I began this chapter with the story of puzzle building with my companion to illustrate one important point though. Fun doesn't always mean club-hopping, movie-watching nights on the town. Some people have fun in quality time with their families. Some people have fun causing chaos. Other people have fun staring at their collection of whatever. For some people, you can put them outside around a bunch of trees and that's all they need. And some people have fun building puzzles. One of the first things we'll need to do in order to get a handle on Dimension 5 is to abandon the idea that fun and play needs to take the forms commonly advertised to us. A major contributor to a sweetheart's sense of inadequacy will be the extent to which they think themselves unable to provide the kind of lifestyle that the partner deserves. "The people on TV are goofing it up ziplining through an exotic animal refuge on the back of a cruise ship, but I can't afford that." And all the images of smiling, extraverted faces socializing over their beers convince women that they should be more strut-sassy, men that they should be more hot-man-object, and all Americans that they should display their social-climbing successes through the selected array of positively valenced activities. Grab your beer, book the vacation, romp across your green lawn at the family picnic and join us in the dream. This is fun, right?

We're all different though. So let's create a working definition of fun that will serve us personally.

Fun is how you voluntarily and enjoyably behave towards an interactant when you're not obligated to do so.

I've recently started using this definition for myself and happen to love it. First, maybe you can see based on this definition that the obligation to have a good time—on a date, at a family gathering, at a compulsory work event—can now officially qualify as NOT fun. You can have fun there if you want, but no one's gonna make you. In order for a thing to be fun here, it *has* to be something you want to do. Secondly, "voluntarily and enjoyably" means that no one is allowed to purchase your sense of fun with their money or their status or anything like that. The realms of your enjoyment are not for sale, and you have the right to reassign your enjoyment to more fun things whenever you want. So when your sweetheart starts trippin' out and the sense of the voluntary is lost in you, we no longer have to be conflicted over whether dealing with them is fun. It's ok if it isn't. There is also the related notion of respect that comes into play, such that a person who pushes you around yet still expects you to have fun with them may now be considered off their rocker.

Respect is where you see someone or something in the way their actions, position, or circumstance suggest that they be seen.

Where people seem to want to be seen in one way but do things to be seen other than that way, they invite your lack of respect in that area. Maybe not your *dis*respect (your <u>active</u> denial of the treatment they ask for), but certainly your lack of respect. In other words, our fun can continue as long as we respect the outlet through which we have it. Once the means to that fun loses our respect for it how it works, our voluntary, enjoyable behavior under those workings loses its foundation. We may begin to have our fun *despite them* rather than with them.

Fun requires the absence of obligation. You *can* have fun in a thing you're obligated to do (like work), but you're typically not obligated to enjoy yourself as you fulfill that obligation. For fun to happen, the enjoyment part needs to be voluntary even if the work part isn't.

We introduced respect into the equation because fun is a fickle beast. In order to have it we need for there to be the potential for an obligation, and that obligation has to be out of the way. But we also need to do something that de-acknowledges the obligation. Then again, the thing we *are* doing for fun needs to have certain specific conditions in order for it to apply. So fun is a voluntary sandwich squeezed between two sets of rules: one set which doesn't apply and the other which we use in order to carry out the fun thing. If any part of this sandwich gets spoiled because someone mixed up the rules with the enjoyment, respect for the sandwich goes down and the fun goes away.

Now what does all this have to do with relationships? If you want to increase the fun in your relationships, you'll need to respect the difference between things that can be obligated and things that can't be obligated. Early in my sexual career I had partners to whom I felt obligated to smash it Dimension 8 and Dimension 1 style. We carried out our affairs doing the advertised fun things for them, but none of the real Dimension 5 things for me. There was only the obligation to constantly entertain them, with no room to discuss my wants. Do you think this was fun? No it wasn't. Having other cats in the bed with you, other dogs in your fight, other snakes on your plane can instantly turn a voluntary exchange into an ego contest between you and the lineup of standards against which you are compared. The secret in Dimension 5 has less to do with what kinds of fun we like to have and more to do with the kinds of fun our partners *let* us have. You can have ripping fun sex with people whose respect for your preferences is obvious. But sex will be no fun if that respect isn't there. Are you seeing each other in the ways that supports how each person wants to be seen? No?

Wha— NO!?

Well then how can you get voluntary action out of *them* when you obligate them to act like someone else?

As a basic rule, if you don't let me show you what I like, I can't fuck you. Hormones aside, someone has to push for my interests when we co-create, and if that co-creation is all about you, you might as well go fuck yourself. Sex for fun is all about how we play and has analogies to the roles we take in play, so that the partner gets to share our toys if they play nicely. As when we were children, play time can often be no holds barred as long as nobody puts an eye out, but the more there is forced imposition of things we aren't interested in, the less likely we are to play enjoyably. Accordingly, play is the route to discovering your Dimension 5 persona, where this dimension's chief benefit is to help you develop your creative talents to their maximum.

Remember why we have bodies? Dimension 5 is where you put your particular reasons to work.

Besides serving as an experience trigger for the broad world, so much of our specific body design is made for the things we play with and the places where it happens. Hey, watch this...BOYOYOING! (...SWIMMING, MAN! That was supposed to be a diving board.) And our bodies bound into action. Highly sensitive bodies favor intellectual or tactile play. Athletic bodies favor physical maneuvering. Big bodies favor big pleasure. Lusty bodies favor new (or more) experiences. You can spot a compatible Dimension 5 partner wherever you spot a person who *would play with <u>you</u>* in person and in the mind, and this is not the same as spotting a partner whom *you* would want to play with. Hormones can get people in trouble on this last point.

Just because a person is hot, doesn't mean you should drop your fun just to join them in theirs. Just because a person has status or access, doesn't mean they're automatically worth your messaging them. After you've observed this kind of thing enough times, you realize you're not the first to want this from them, and it really is valuable if they want to join you in your play too. This isn't so much about who makes the first move as it is about who seems to show interest in the other's space when even the tiniest sample moves are made. In general, if you feel like chasing new company because you're feeling lonely or unsupported in the old, your approaching someone else to fill the void will install "a cure for loneliness" as one of your Dimension 9 motivators; there's a good chance you'll attract someone who presents you with "loneliness" as a central issue. Let's hope you're not asking for something you don't want. Hopefully the loneliness theme will come in the form of a mercifully quick nonresponse.

Your play is yours. Dropping it in order to pull someone else may work for some, but not for most. Try to respect your own company before asking someone else to respect it for you.

Let's Play

So what do you like to do for fun? No, really. When the opportunities for a night out and an occasional trip are unavailable, what do you do? This is less about the activity and more about the projection. Do you stay in your own internal space (Self), interact with something (Other), or engage abstract collections of ideas outside of yourself (World)? Do you like dealing with things (Earth and Water) or processes (Fire and Air)? Do you like topics that can be observed by all (Earth and Air) or events that must be interpreted subjectively (Fire and Water)? Whatever your voluntarily enjoyable preference, know that the person you seek to have fun with needs to enable this broad dimension in you. Anything less won't be nearly as fun. This gets us into the territory of using people as a means to an end.

The ways in which we play can get massively exotic. From Duplo to Lego to Knime nodes; from jumping jacks to cheer team to interpretive dance. More than any other dimension, practiced creative play is our means to talented self-worth, and the irony is that this same dimension which would drive us to have sex with whomever, would also encourage us to abstain from sex while we grow new skills independent of our partner's understanding. The more complex your play the more complex the playmate you require, if not in the same field then at least on the same mastery level. If this doesn't happen, you might still maintain things by donating your skills down to them. If even this doesn't happen then you may need to find balance in other relationship areas like the shared world you create. But one of the chief rules of Dimension 5 is that your playmate needs to enable your play. Obviously. Squashing your dreams acts as a pretty basic play killer, as does failing to make room for the more complex stages of your growth. Actually there's at least one very common case where this rule doesn't apply: If you're simply willing to give up your creative dimension in order to preserve the relationship as you understand it, the relationship may endure even if your own development stops.

Dimension 5 Sex

To those of us for whom the advertised modes of play don't easily apply, good dimension 5 sex may require a better understanding of how you have fun outside of the bedroom. Those situations where you can honestly say you had a fun time mirrors the kinds of sex that you'll find playful.

- Socializing (Air)
- Emotional or Intuitive (Water)
- Action based (Fire)
- Structure based (Earth)

- Internal to your [Self]
- Done against an [Other]
- Approached in the [World]

We're going to talk about how to translate your creative options into sex and vice versa, but before we do that we'll need to chop up sex into its components for easier conversion.

So when I'm not writing on interpersonal dynamics I'm usually working on some kind of data analysis. There are different kinds of algorithms that exist out there and a couple of them involve cramming all the stuff you're working with, things and processes, into a single piece of information. We can think of sex-mode as being a kind of information block on your behaviors. It has various options for you and your partners as well as countless options for how you and your partner interact. To translate a behavioral pattern like a hobby into sex we'll first need a basic estimate of how many factors we're looking at. Let's say that you have 12 dimensions, your partner has 12, and your setting has 12 (Self's, Other's, and World's worlds have 12 dimensions each.) Also, each of your worlds has 12 options within it representing the flavor of the dimension. Some people wield power to communicate themselves, others do it to uncover facts. So we have 12 x 12 three times or 144^3. That's way too many factors, so we'll reduce the number by counting only the data pieces we're concerned with:

3 scopes to an actor x 4 modes x (3 scopes to an intended target x 4 modes per target) $^{\wedge\ 1\ you\ +\ 1\ interactant\ +\ 1\ setting}$)

If we think of this whole thing as a giant average "special move" which sums up your creative dynamic, then taking these 3+4+3+4+1+1+1 variables will give us everything we need to scrunch your hobby into a style. That's 17 variables. And here's what we get:

Interaction Item *Consider what you love to do for fun:*	The Author's Structure-building example
1. Self-Orientation/Openness/ Hedonism. What do you love most about the interaction?	The ability to build dynamic, interactive structures that no one else can build

Dimension 5: Sex to Mirror Your Hobbies

Write your answer here:	
2. Interaction/Focus/**Directed Intention**. How much does this activity involve things which you influence directly?	A lot
3. Abstraction/Need for Cognition/ **Contextualizing**. How much of it is meant to be broadcast to the world right then or later on?	All of it, at first only to people who appreciate the work, later to everyone everywhere.
4. Inner-Fire/ **Masculinity**. How much does your own intentional effort matter to you?	With people, not much. I like to be the tool through which the creativity flows naturally. With work, a lot. I do strongly prefer to create upon the unknown though. The known bores me, and I have little to do there. (The last part favors the form of a biological male while the first part favors an interpersonally less assertive one.)
5. Inner-Earth/Neuroticism/ Form-**Insistence**/Tool Use. How much do you require tangible bodies or objects in the interaction?	The pieces must be pre-made. A pre-set list of possible building, a preset group of blocks, nodes, or dynamics. Building shit completely from scratch makes the artist in me angry.

6. Inner-Air/**Extraversion**. How much communication do you require from yourself during the interaction?	None. I like to get immersed in it, and in doing so am most comfortable with the internal monologue off.
7. Inner-Water/Agreeable-ness/ **Femininity**. How much does the closeness to others matter to you?	Not so much. I lose focus on the thing itself and space out on the vibe. If others are around, fine as long as they don't distract me. If not, that's usually better.
8. Other's Self/Anti-Inner Fire/ **Gender**. How complemen-tary does your partner's receipt of your Inner-Fire/effort need to be?	Complete. If I decide to do something I expect it to work the first time. If it's buggy, and I haven't gotten attached to it. I'll make plans to start a new file/city/creation immediately.
9. Other's Other/Partner Number/**Monogamy**. Does the interactant require *you* as their Other (Mono-type; you are their chief interactant), a *group* as their Other (socioPoly-type: you share them; them as group-immersed), or a single	I refuse to play network games, but also refuse to step into the same river twice. The thing should present infinite possibilities using only a few pre-made pieces. So having an additional "infinite principle" is really important to me. Me + the thing + its own

stimulant *internal to themselves* which you facilitate (modPoly-type: they share you; you plus their principle = their interactant)?	infinite source of possibility. So I'd say my partner should be modPoly: the partner (building block) needs her own partner or principle that precedes me.
10. Other's World/**Exhibitionism**. Are you more or less comfortable having the interactant broadcast the event to everyone?	Yep. What I don't tell people near me, things like this book will tell to everyone everywhere. My goal is to have aired everything I've built, secret or not, by the time I die.
11. Other-Fire/Your **Dominance**. How submissive to your influence would you prefer your interactant to be?	I only play games I can win and win big in, and rarely on hard mode. The process needs to be very malleable in order for me to like it.
12. Other-Earth/**Foreignness**. How close to your trained class of experience should the interactant be (A reliable habit or a source of the unfamiliar)?	Never the same city twice. If possible, I like to learn new rules even from very old games, so foreign results are a must.
13. Other-Air/**Magnetism**. Do you prefer your	I like little known gems (or less mainstream ones), and prefer to remain one myself.

partners to be mainly attractors of others' communication or should they bring out the attractor in you?	But I like the creations I make using those tools to be epic and well-known. I suppose the whole should be *much* bigger than the parts, and it's even more special if the parts are small, weird or underestimated.
14. Other-Water/Other-Independence/**Community**. How much does the interactant lean on external supporters for its basic definition?	For occasional mods okay, but *required* network play? No way. I don't do unbounded sets—only bounded sets with unbounded combinations. The interactant can definitely stand alone, and is better doing so.
15. **Role**. Archetype. Which of the basic 12 dimensions best describes your role in the interaction?	I am an Architect, Dimension 10 (a later chapter)
16. **Goal**. Which of the basic 12 dimensions best describes the thing you're doing or person you're interacting with?	She is (or they are) A Unique Society, Dimension 11 (later)
17. **Frequency** Setting. Which of the basic 12 dimensions best describes the character of information getting passed back and forth during the interaction?	It entails Structure or Inspiration, Dimensions 6 (later) or 12

Conclusion: The Author as a system-monument builder (hobby)
Strong need to feel in control. Won't be pushed or directed. Doesn't need public approval for self or partner but wants it for the total interaction. Either multiple partners or highly intellectual (networked) ones; partners need to know themselves well enough to be past needing correction and onto some grand seeking. Partner should love being structured by something outside of themselves, should know how to fuel themselves, and should be rare or exceptional in some way compared to everyone else. Tools are okay. Sex should be a joint discovery. The more absorption the better. Routine is no good. Being held responsible for shaping the other's experience is no good. From a different background is very good. Like an always changing city, the preferred partner is always growing. The setting must be stably structured or coherently ordered.

(Sounds like a personals ad doesn't it?)

To help you use the above table, I've entered my own responses in a sample column. Since I like city building games and structuring systems for fun, you can see how the chain of descriptors produces a pretty decent summary of likes. I'm a bit of an exhibitionist if you haven't noticed by now, but only when I think people would benefit from what I have to show them: Even though the conclusion doesn't look that fancy, I kid you not when I tell you that the above kind of sex for me is as fun as it gets. All of that from a non-sexual hobby. In case you didn't fill in your answers above, I've included an extra table below.

Interaction Item *Consider what you love to do for fun:*	
1. Self-Orientation/Openness/ **Hedonism**. What do you love most about the interaction?	
2. Interaction/Focus/**Directed Intention**. How much does this activity involve things which you influence directly?	
3. Abstraction/Need for	

Cognition/**Contextualizing**. How much of it is meant to be broadcast to the world right then or later on?	
4. Inner-Fire/**Masculinity**. How much does your own intentional effort matter to you?	
5. Inner-Earth/Neuroticism/Form-**Insistence**/Tool Use. How much do you require tangible bodies or objects in the interaction?	
6. Inner-Air/**Extraversion**. How much communication do you require from yourself during the interaction?	
7. Inner-Water/Agreeableness/**Femininity**. How much does the closeness to others matter to you?	
8. Other's Self/Anti-Inner Fire/**Gender**. How complementary does your partner's receipt of your Inner-Fire/effort need to be?	
9. Other's Other/Partner Number/**Monogamy**. Does the interactant require *you* as their Other (Mono-type; you are their chief interactant), a *group* as their Other (socioPoly-type: you share them; them as group-immersed), or a single stimulant *internal to themselves* which you facilitate (modPoly-type: they share you; you plus their principle = their interactant)?	
10. Other's World/**Exhibitionism**. Are you more or less comfortable having the	

interactant broadcast the event to everyone	
11. Other-Fire/Your **Dominance**. How submissive to your influence would you prefer your interactant to be?	
12. Other-Earth/**Foreignness**. How close to your trained class of experience should the interactant be (A reliable habit or a source of the unfamiliar)?	
13. Other-Air/**Magnetism**. Do you prefer your partners to be mainly attractors of others' communication or should they bring out the attractor in you?	
14. Other-Water/Other-Independence/**Community**. How much does the interactant lean on external supporters for its basic definition?	
15. **Role**. Archetype. Which of the basic 12 dimensions best describes your role in the interaction?	
16. **Goal**. Which of the basic 12 dimensions best describes the thing you're doing or person you're interacting with?	
17. **Frequency** Setting. Which of the basic 12 dimensions best describes the character of information getting passed back and forth during the interaction?	
Conclusion	

Although we could have said, "I want someone who loves underwater basket weaving just like me" and left it at that, we would have missed out on all the power, personality, and exchange dynamics which are trapped in that hobby as a form. You like clubbing? The activity above, chops clubbing up into a set of variables that you can use piece by piece, including some of the more hidden variables like gender and hedonism. Many people have told me that tables like the above constitute over-intellectualizing, but you don't have to use the table if you don't want to. The thing is, though, for any of us who have ever found our partners on the basis of fun only to break up with them later when they became no fun, it's not always because either we or the other changed at all. It's often because the fun we thought we were having in the beginning wasn't actually the kind that the deeper kid in us would want—only a conveniently available, socialized option. The table above is intended to help you break that packaged hobby into a set of dimensions that actually describe your dynamics in the long run, allowing you to see more easily what that fun partner should really look like. Even if the club burned down.

If you were honest with yourself, your final list of hobby descriptors probably won't follow the advertised model. There may be some road-tripping in there, but even on a basic level the advertised model just doesn't describe enough. For readers who think I pulled this stuff out of the air, I didn't. It's actually a rearranged combination of

- 4 of the Big-Five personality factors
- 1 construct called Need for Cognition
- 2 Interpersonality axes: Communion (Warmth) and Agency (Dominance)
- 3 sex dimensions
- 2 sex role Interpersonality axes
- 2 country culture axis dimensions
- 3 Locus of Control factors

The psychology research is deep and interesting, and now we can all use it to happily shag anyone we want. Take your conclusions and get out there!

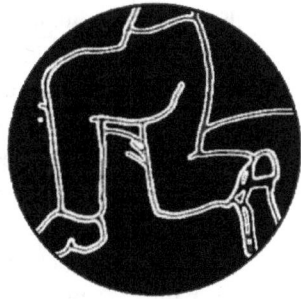

11 DIMENSION 6: *Called to Duty*

Duty sex: arguably the lamest sex we can possibly have. When your lover wants it and you don't...When you've got other things on your mind, bills to pay, plants to water...When faking it is your only hope, there is **Dimension 6**.

Is there anything redeeming about the sex that happens under contractual mandate? Of course there is. Duty sex may not be the most popular kind of sex, but for ages of humans we could guess that it's probably far and away the most frequent type of sex on the planet. Always has been and always will be. For people who've already gotten all of those first surprises out of the way and finally settled into kind of routine, Dimension 6 offers a brand of stamp-the-document regularity that keeps the bodies grinding even after the childlike anticipation has vanished. I asked the guardians what to write about this one and here's what they said:

What you call duty sex is the regular maintenance of the creative spark between partners. Or we should say regularized. Not every sexual encounter can be exceptionally thrilling, and for those whose only purpose is to reassure the participants of the relationship's continued physical and intimate validity, this type of sex is available [image of an old hat].

So why is it that humans frown upon sex for the sake of the relationship? We don't have an answer to that, but we do wish to say that the purpose of duty sex is often to keep common ground within the relationship. To the extent that humans continue to hold the capacity for pleasure, there remains the possibility of being creatively stimulated by someone, somewhere. But now imagine a relationship in which the partners no longer seek to get that stimulation from each other. Imagine the loss, the bitterness that some people feel when they no longer think themselves appealing to the partner. While much of the sex you describe in this book is done for selfish or self-focused reasons, "duty sex" as you call it stands alone in its complete dedication to another beyond oneself. Here there is no sharing (7), no steering (8), and no self-promotion (5). Of the four dimensions dedicated to engaging the Other, only Dimension 6 is interested in finding common ground between what the partner needs and what you can provide them.

We handle duty sex in the same way that we handle work. Once there, we adopt a pattern of action aimed at getting the job done. But there is an interesting connection between this dimension and the person's general health: While the things we do for a paycheck consist of the generic services we provide to the outer world broadly, our service to that world remains a parallel to the kinds of service we provide to anything that maintains our form's reification in this life. If the job gives you a formed shell in society, the body gives you a formed shell in this life. Your obligation to maintain your shells manifests both through the job and through the bodily health, though the two levels are clearly not the same. Even though the state of the body does not always reflect the state of the world-sponsored work, the state of the body does always reflect the state of the mass of responsibilities that a person believes she faces in making herself known to the world as a useful citizen. In this way, physical ailments tell us where certain sections of an otherwise normal life script must be specially redirected towards our relationships to the systems that support us.

Thank you, by the way OML for writing this, no wonder the angels have increasingly begun to seek you as their scribe. We believe that the information contained in this book will do wonders for the people seeking to better their lives through relationships with others, and will gladly tell you more about this realm you call level 6.

In reality the people in this life seek different forms of experience, not always happiness. The clarity with which they *can* seek is additionally hindered by the operations performed on top of once simple job duties. In a society where there is much metadata on systems aimed at sustaining those systems for their own sake, and where the aim of benefitting the individual worker is lost, the role of maintenance sex between partners who can rely on each other is even more important than ever. That's because the job is no longer a source of reliable identity, but rather a tool for the use of institutions to funnel capital among themselves. But that is changing. In intimate relationships, the people find ways of delving deep into each other's' needs that validate the soul beneath the working shell, so that for many, duty sex is more real as a reflection of the person's work than his actual work is. I may have been hired as a teacher, but my administrative responsibilities and legal duties prevent me from truly teaching. But I can't just fly to a less bureaucratic country. So where can I really teach if only the post in front of me exists as a viable option? What if my dream is to help people, but the grant cycle prevents me from truly doing that? Where can I go? For such a sense of purpose in the larger world—where an individual can bring his skills to bear in ordered, coordinated cooperation with others, a person needs meaning in the work he does no matter what it is. This is true of work at the job, work at home, or work on the body. Without meaning, his world becomes full of wasted effort on nothing but noise. Alas, all he has is his partner's duty sex to remind him of what that work should have looked like if he had had all of his proper public options truly available to him.

You can take it from here. So ends the lesson.

So it turns out that Dimension 6 is one of the types that best reflects our spirit of service to the world around us. Given that the same world

sustains us, it's not so much out of obligation, but out of continued energy exchange with the food we eat and dispose of, the air we breathe in and exhale, and the events we sponsor and experience that service through work becomes a natural part of the cycle. If life gives us fuel through Dimension 12, we convert that fuel into a byproduct filtered through our own personality and send it back out through the work we do for others.

Often when I read astrology charts, people ask me what the chart says about their job. I always give them the same answer. "The chart won't tell you what your job is, but it will give you a really good look at the process you employ during work. For readers who are curious, asteroids like Ceraskia, Ottegebe, Arachne, and the king of work Moultona are great indicators, as well as Saturn, Selene and the Midheaven. The thing about these indicators is that they only tell you the character of what they represent in your life. They don't tell the form, and they don't tell your attitude towards that form. The harmony or discontentment you feel in your work is up to you. The guardians indicated that work is one of the strongest areas of our lives dedicated to other's fulfillment, and that our health is a reflection of how we see our responsibilities to others. Changes in our health significantly change our interactions with others, and prompt those others to deal with us in ways that are special. So Dimension 6 has two sides: our service to the world and our interactants' directed responses in light of us. In intimate exchanges we have the opportunity to practice how we act in full interdependence with another. In ill health we are compelled to address how we handle any burdens which we may believe have been placed on us by other forces—be they God, other people, or our own nature broadly.

I've spent large sections of my life evading committed relationships, and typically don't try very hard to make room for things that don't advance my scholarship. In terms of Dimension 6, I might be said to serve independently, at my own will, and through complicated means. To establish an effective Dimension 6 relationship, a person needs to have some sense of duty-sharing towards and from another, and in cases where he doesn't have both sides, he can be said to "not make room" for a daily, long-term relationship. Coming and going as you please, cat-style, isn't enough. Letting others come and go as they please, corner store-style, isn't enough either. Our challenge here is not so much to learn how to build a Dimension 6 relationship, but to build a relationship in general. Adding intimacy as a factor, we would also like for that relationship to possess that quality which assures us of the partner's interest in us even when we're no longer new and shiny.

Dimension 6 Sex

We'll start our discussion of sex in this dimension early so that we can move on to more interesting aspects of it afterwards. Your attitude towards duty sex parallels your attitude towards duty. That much we could have guessed. When you give yourself in service to another, you prioritize their needs even if you don't really have any. We could have guessed that too. Of course this doesn't mean having sex when you don't want to. But it might mean having sex when the Other wants to and you're *indifferent*, if your aim is to keep them happy. This is a glass-half-full matter which, over time, ends up having major implications for the partnership. Will you do things that are useful for the other, harmless to you, but not directly useful to you either? Would you want or expect them to do the same if the situation were reversed? It's the same old golden rule as always. Duty sex may not by itself present you with any overt thrills, but it is precisely for this reason that it is so valuable in a long-term physical relationship where the partner's timing doesn't always match. Again, this doesn't mean you should have sex when you don't want to. But there is an element of giving in this kind of thing which scatters seeds all over the rest of the relationship.

I want it, but you don't care. You have a headache. You're tired. Alright.

You want it but I don't care. After I watch this whatever-it-is. Maybe later. Fine, right? No harm in turning indifference into a solid "don't bother me," right?

I know this subject could get touchy, but it doesn't have to. If you don't want to do it, say no. But if you're *truly indifferent*, consider a yes. Not because I'm a male who likes his sex. (That's not valid, and not even close to a reason for me.) Not because I have old fashioned views. (I don't.) But because I, like you, have honestly run into too many selfish partners who wanted one thing from their mate but wouldn't give that same thing *to* their mate. They wanted their partner to act on the former's whim, but wouldn't roll off the couch unless the partner's wishes expressly benefitted them. So you don't do duty sex? The only sex you have is sex that benefits you? Even in times when it doesn't matter either way to you? And how would you like a partner who treated *you* that way? We're all entitled to our approaches, of course. And if that approach has helped you find fulfillment, I suppose you should stay with it...

But if the one-sided approach to pleasure is something you do AND you've been able to keep up the happiness level in a long-term physical relationship, then you're part of a rare breed.

Your approach to duty sex is related to your approach to work. It's only as terrible as you make it. There's no science to it. All you need to do is show up. And on that note let me share with you a conversation I had with a partner of mine:

> Her: You don't look so enthusiastic about this. If you don't want to—
>
> Me: Nah, I'm good. I'm up for it.
>
> Her: Reeally. Be honest now. You're not in the mood.
>
> Me: No, I'm not, but—
>
> Her: Then just forget about it. Let's just do something else.

> Me: Hey, come here. I'm not in the mood for it, but I am in the mood for you. Because I love you (kiss), it's whatever you want.

That's it. There's no need to be mean, and no need to box your partner in with an emphasis on your own selfishness. If you're *truly indifferent*, and if it would make your partner happy, consider saying yes to them. Being able to do things for them that may not benefit you will go a long way in keeping the relationship strong. Long-term successfully partnered pairs already know this. Many of the rest of us—still trekking through the dating wilderness—don't.

As far as your duty sex persona is concerned, it works the way your work persona does. Rather than go into details regarding this, let's just agree that if there are ways to develop a better attitude toward a thing that circumscribes so much of our lives, maybe we should try it. There really are people without partners who would kill for a shot at duty sex, just as there are some people without jobs who would love a shot at its obligations. Duty shows us where others are counting on us. And even though I truly love my freedom more than most people in my circle, I really think that so many people's inconsiderate brush off of others' wants in the name of selfish utility is just a damned shame. So much bitterness. So much selfishness. All because we won't give unless we're paid back. And the people who do this aren't even happy with themselves. What's the point of all that ego?

Using Dimension 6 to Build a New Relationship

If the secret to Dimension 6 sex is simply to show up when your partner wants it (when it won't put you out), and for you to be there for them with an attitude of love, then the broader secret to even obtaining a daily-duty style partner works in the same way. My thoughts on this topic are the same as my thoughts on any request: If it won't put me out and it will make the other person happy, I do it. Because I can, and because doing so opens me to something beyond my narrow view which Life wants to give me in infinite supply. We give service to the world in an attitude of love towards the realm in which we donate our skills. If we love the trade even without the pay, if our aim is to give our best with a personal investment in the quality of work we do, then the nature of the work becomes our partner.

Now in my mind this all sounds very conformist. If I work at McDonalds where there is a definite process for doing things, how can I possibly give personal investment in my work? But it's not the task alone that matters, it's also the attitude. It's the relationships we form with our peers, the outlook we bring to the things we're asked to do, and the satisfaction with which we view the chain of choices of which McDonalds is a part. You don't necessarily have to be happy with where you are, but you can choose to be happy with where you're going and how you're getting there. Where you are is a part of that. Yes the pay is important, but thoughts about the pay don't have to dominate our views. Our work is our character directed out to everyone. A good attitude towards it helps us see all duty as an opportunity to be useful to everything around us.

For people still in search of that great relationship, Dimension 6 shows us what kinds of dynamic we might hope for. However we approach work, we may expect to approach with a similar attitude in our daily dealings with a partner. However we got hired, we can expect to initiate those daily dealings with that partner. As stated in an earlier chapter, we may not need a partner if the most important thing currently in our lives would fare better without one, but in general our ability to support a long-term partner is circumscribed by our ability to accommodate someone else in our daily routine. This includes changes in what kinds of feedback we receive regarding our choices, what kinds of inputs we take for information and health, and what kinds of expectations we have for making a worldly impression. Clearly supporting a partner can be complicated business for those of us accustomed to having our worlds to ourselves, but the overall idea is that the addition of a partner to one's life rests upon our ability to successfully merge another's behaviors into our own agenda.

You can attract a partner using a simple array of five steps. The partner may not be ideal, but they will be a "companionized" version of the situation you're currently in. Here's how you do it.

1. **Look to the source of your need to have a partner.** Is it because you're lonely? Excited to share? Seeking help towards some goal? Note your main motivation for wanting a partner right now. It might well be different from your reasons for wanting a partner in general.

2. **Ask yourself what qualities you want to be most salient in this partner.** You can ask, and often you'll get everything you ask for. As mentioned before, however, there are unlimited combinations of things you won't have the time or interest in asking for, and these will shape those qualities of the partner which design themselves automatically.

3. **Seek out the context where that partner is normally found.** This is the hardest step, because people seeking partners often don't know that they should look in jobs, books, movies, purchases, or laws they already follow— things they already have easy access to—in order to locate their mate. They usually just look in places with other people. Especially for a chronically single person, it pays to look in places which actually populate your life at the moment, since so much of what you have the immediate potential to experience is already captured in your *present* array of experiences. There in the future you'll find a pattern of things you wished for and forms you wished them into, with your own cognition serving as the filter through which the experiences you wanted were finally given a form that you could live with.

   Previously you may have thought that certain experiences were better captured by a job or a hobby, but through this practice you may find that a *person* constituted a better form. Or maybe not. In the end, you almost certainly already have what you're looking for because your mind has to draw that image of the goal from somewhere. Your job is to find the thing in your life which currently houses this pattern. Your dream partner might actually *be* a TV show you're currently watching with which you interact in the same way that you would your partner. Locate the <u>dynamic</u> in what's around you, not the person at the meetup who's *not* around you. It sounds weird, I know. But you'll need to try it before you conclude it won't work for you.

4. The next step to attracting a partner is actually the easiest of the five: **Listen to what the form you found tells you about what it wants from you, then give it**. This is a matter of effort applied to whatever situation houses your form, and also has implications for your broader psychology which has stacked a chain of causes in order to put your wanted mate in this form. You can consider that there were reasons for you getting to the point that you have gotten to, so listening to a situation is not as crazy as it sounds. All you're doing is replaying the chain of events that put you where you are, and processing that chain in a way that can be described using human dynamics. You're not really "listening." You're really just surveying a pattern and retelling a communicative story to yourself.

5. The last step in attracting a partner is to **receive the information that the formed situation gives you as a regular contribution in your life**. Recalling that a person's partner is really just a package of energy in which he temporarily stores certain psychological patterns of his own, receiving information regarding the people who know the fruits of their labor, you can see how the situation which has locked up the qualities of

your ideal partner can actually be an ongoing, regular contributor to the life you normally lead. By receiving the information which that situation has to offer, you effectively condition your psychology to receive from a humanized version of that same thing. Accordingly, you'll have access to a partner by following all the steps required to transform an existing dynamic in to a human one, and we can actually apply this situation to any circumstances you encounter, not just romantic. But you absolutely <u>have to</u> receive, don't just reject. Otherwise you may attract a partner who truly doesn't need you to receive their efforts. And that's as good as no partner at all.

As always, it helps to ask whether you even need a partner. Dimension 6 is especially useful for getting one, but if you're not seriously in a position to start sharing all of your hopes and fears, you may not like what you get. People who hit on you uninvited. People who set you up as friends but then punish you for not being mates in the way that they wanted. People who cling to you but then look for faults in you as a means of affirming themselves—any of these may come as a result of "partnerizing" a dynamic in your life when you should have just let it stay as a job.

Conclusion

Dimension 6 may not be the most impressive dimension, but it is THE dimension for establishing and maintaining daily routine. Accordingly, it is also the Dimension you use for inviting new romantic relationships into your life. Although the secrets to Dimension 6 aren't very secret, the idea of acting for a job the way you would if that job were a person remains more relevant to Dimension 6 than any other dimension. We're not looking for thrills, only for practical use for ourselves in the world. And although some people might find this disappointing, it's actually this dimension which is most directly responsible for whether the relationship lives or dies upon either partner's selfishness. Generosity is encouraged. Generosity with time, with resources, and with shared ideas regardless of the form in which the long-term exchange plays out.

In the end, Dimension 6 is all about what we can do for others. Its tests are simple, but profound. When it comes to this dimension, everything we do is dictated by what someone else needs, and the secret to great performance lies in tending to those needs. Beneath all of this though, lies the extent to which we can still care about our partners even though they've asked us to do something which doesn't directly please us. Can we rise to the challenge, or will we render them nothing more than a useless pleasure object to be transactionally called upon at our own convenience? It depends on whether we are truly ready for shared happiness in our lives, or just working out issues. Dimension 6 challenges us to alter our long-term plans by checking to see if we are really capable of including someone else in them. Exercised correctly we may attract someone more beautiful in spirit and fulfilling in body than we could ever imagine ourselves. Exercised wrongly, Dimension 6 may only invite trouble. Much of this trouble will be related to us attempting to bring an entire life into our circle with no intention of benefitting it—only to selfishly alleviate our own loneliness at the moment. Your reasons for entering the realm of duty really do matter.

12 DIMENSION 4: *I Want to Feel*

Dimension 4 is the last of the fairly conservative dimensions, after which Dimensions 2, 3, 10, and 11 will take us into more exotic lands. If Dimension 6 was about the kinds of exchanges we enter when the partner wants it and we're neutral, then Dimension 4 is about the kinds of exchanges we enter when we want it and our partners are neutral...or unavailable. On the other side of a partner's duty lies the one who calls the partner to duty. "Fulfill me!" says the **Dimension 4** person. Here in the space of Self-Water it's all about the exchanges we seek for satisfying our internally felt **inclinations**. It's conservative in that it represents one of our basic reasons for seeking sex at all. But then again, it's kind of not. Dimension 4 is also the one most heavily associated with masturbation and fantasy. It is also a more toned-down version of the "proclivities" family (1, 3, 9, and 11), where you want something just because your subconscious says so. Taking our cue from Nina Hartley, our ability to get pleasure from sex is ultimately on us, not on our partners. In Self-Water we'll learn how to take back control of our own satisfaction from all those external sources, so that we can healthily, unashamedly own the wants that are truly pleasing to us. This will also prepare us for the chapters to come. Get ready to own yourself. It'll be worth it.

When we're hungry, we eventually eat. When we're tired, we eventually sleep. When we're living, we eventually die. When we're horny, that depends...but why? It's because of social shaming, probably. Since mature, mainstream discussions of sexuality are heavily partner-centered and thick with prescriptions for approved social practices, we're taught that our fantasies should mostly involve titillating people-images, emotional fuzzies, and maybe love-stories. We're taught that the ultimate fulfillment of our desires surely must be left to a socially validating partner, a rich lifestyle, or a carefree social event. And if you masturbate, it's probably because you can't get a partner or you have some secretly deviant side that you struggle to hide from the rest of us normal people. All of this is training.

Something internal to us and natural to our biology has controls installed upon it from external sources, and from then on we believe that the chief acceptable routes to fulfillment of our wants must be through those controls. To help this along, we happily shame others for defying those controls; we eagerly shame our friends for associating with those others. Unsurprisingly this is the same process through which dehumanization outgroups is enforced. **Dehumanization** is where you treat others with less than the full array of human privileges that you would give to groups you identify with. You know, "those people." "A good [so and so] doesn't do what they do, and if you listen to or associate with those people at all, you risk not being a good [so and so]." Dimension 4 quickly introduces us to the vast world of prejudices associated with how people think, where your ingroup becomes the thought police and the outgroup becomes some kind of moral or psychological enemy.

A discussion of our fantasies and how we satisfy them needs to begin with a discussion of what we think is allowed—mainly for ourselves. It begins with a discussion of the punishments we levy upon things for breaching those expectations—mainly on ourselves.

> In the worst relationship I ever had, I worked with someone with whom I fought nonstop. But the day I ended it was the day she said to me, "all that [pagan stuff you talk] goes against my religion." Combined with a much longer backstory which I won't bore you with here, I said to myself within minutes "We're building a project which accepts all people. Fighting I can do. Blanket intolerance I can't. She is truly a bad person." And that was it. This person was one of only two really bad people I've ever met. Despite all of the other misunderstandings related to how I showed openness and how she showed structure, I wanted to make it work. I also wanted her to want to make it work. But intolerance for others' perspectives when you never even bother to ask about those perspectives or see if you've understood them? You'll struggle to make those others want to give you anything. Meanwhile, you'll only poison yourself and your ingroup with anger. The very next day after I ended the exchange I was greeted with a newer and better one, enjoyed the most peaceful outing I'd enjoyed with someone in a long time, and the stress of the previous months went away. I haven't experienced that level of angry energy since. In anyone.

As we noted in the Dimension 9 chapter, people will answer you with *their* understanding of what you did—not with *your* understanding of what you did. And we do the same when we shame others for operating outside of our moral or mental standards. We'll struggle to receive from those others all the packages of experience they possess, which we need to complete ourselves. Nowhere is this more evident than in the desires you allow yourself to have...and the ones you struggle against in secret.

Returning full circle to the chapter on "I love you," our blocking of others' good when it really is good will only confuse us subconsciously. We want to be supremely and faithfully devoted but demonize Muslims. We want order in our civic lives but demonize the government. We want epic pleasure in our lives but demonize those liberated people. That culture which does what they do are demons; but if people who looked like us did it, we'd sometimes want to do *exactly* what they do—or at least try it. Confusing. Psychologically confusing. And when we're confused in our personal rules, we're angry, conflicted, stressed and bitter. Those people shouldn't be able to get away with it, but they *do* get away with it as if Life's telling us all "it's not that bad." But it must be bad. Life is wrong, my clique is right. It's confusing. We'll need to get over this stuff in order to make it through these next five dimensions.

Opening the Fantasy Life

As much as I'd love to just jump in and say let your fantasies free, I know it's not that simple. The subconscious in many of us is like a fortress reinforced over decades spent roaming the familiar. So your fantasies, not surprisingly, will tend to look like stuff you already know and have already accepted—just slightly beyond your reach. They won't be filled with things you lack the proper framework for. Given that, the following exercise may be useful. I'll ask you to do this without judgment towards what you'll write, without guilt towards yourself, and take only 10 seconds to do it.

PLEASE get a timer now, along with a little piece of paper and something to write with. Set the timer for 10 seconds. Turn the page once you're ready.

Take 10 seconds to list all the groups <u>you judge</u> which have done you <u>no wrong</u>.

Now that you have that list, go back and add the following: List the thing that each group has, which you don't think it's fair that they have. (There's no time limit. If you need to think about it, go ahead.)

And now for the important part: Add the traits you wrote to the list of things you want your preferred <u>Dimension 7</u> partner (The Lovemaker) to give to you.

This exercise is powerful. I had two groups on my list. One group had the trait "unquestioned favor." People seemed to side with them no matter how much wrong they did or how much right they didn't do. So I wrote that I wanted my preferred partner to give me unquestioned favor too. The other group had a trait called "Happy-go-lucky lockout." Not only did I add this to my partner list, but I also realized that I myself was (and still am) guilty of it. It may take some time for you to internalize your list and really think about what it means for where you are in your relationships (and not just your romantic ones). It may take a little longer to decide what you want to do about all this. Note, though, that this exercise is not about the groups you judge, but rather the expressive patterns *you associate* with those groups in your own mind. If you go out of your way and dedicate your energy to judging them instead of just letting them slide out as a topic, it's conceivable that you have some psychological investment in how they're able to do what they do. We want that tendency to invest energy in them to benefit your world, not subtract from it. Adding the judged groups' processes to your wish list for partner donations (from them to you) is a one way to turn this kind of judgment around in yours and your ingroup's favor.

We have one more exercise. Set your timer for 1 minute now. This one is harder.

You've had such bad experiences with people of certain classes that you dislike the entire class. List them now.

Now that you have that list, go back and list the thing that you associate with each group, which is negative enough that it shouldn't be done in your world. (There's no time limit. If you need to think about it, go ahead.)

You may have noticed certain themes repeating on your list. Here's the important part: If ever you decided to apply your efforts to a broader cause in the world, the traits you listed would be the things your efforts stand against.

Add [the intention of working against these traits] to the list of things you would want to do in cooperation with the partner you attract.

Finally, if there is a general consistency in the physical or behavioral appearance of the group you've just described, consider the form this appearance represents to be your base of operations from which you and your partner will build this work. Go back to the chapter on body parts if you need to.

If for example you seemed to have a thing against skinny model types, groups that limit the entry of others might be the base group from which you and the partner do your joint work. If you seemed to have a thing against the buff male look, forward asserters of partner defense (something like possessive groups—male or female) might be the base group from which your work starts.

The **base group** comprises the place, behavioral culture, or the original source of resources you and your partner will use to build your joint efforts.

We often get upset with classes of people whose members continually serve us with a certain kind of experience. Psychologically, we associate the perceived form of these people with a particularly uncomfortable idea. The form is where it comes from. The idea is the thing we stand against. The point of this exercise is for you to use that psychological analog to re-impower yourself rather than simply being burdened by a class you can't change. The form isn't the problem. Chineseness, Richness, Republicanness, and Hip Hopness don't just fall out of the sky and harass you. These are frameworks through which people who listed them might feel harassed. That is, they are contexts.

Within those contexts, we have the actual type of experience that weighs us down. The experience will probably never sit right with you on principle, but actively working against it with the help of someone else will feel much better than your getting beat up by it. In your own mind, beating yourself up using people who don't know a thing about you isn't very nice. It isn't very empowering either.

I'll also note that once you start doing the work, your chances of running into discord at the hands of those groups will likely drop dramatically. That's because you will have effectively installed healthy, self-consistent ways of handling the issues you listed. Instead of trying to erase the problem, psychologically you would have solved it.

Okay, so now we've taken things that make us uncomfortable and folded them into our relationship agenda.

Groups we judge unfairly, possess those things we want to receive *unconditionally* from our partners

—perhaps unfairly in others' eyes.

Groups we've come to dislike from person-to-person experience indicate the types of tools we and our partners will use to jointly work to address whatever that experience is, and we'll do it together in the broader world.

Thus we've done a little bit of house-cleaning in our psychologies. The subconscious seldom gets clean overnight, but at least we've located several of the land mines that otherwise would have greeted us in the fantasy world.

In the Mood

Any number of things can prompt us to seek sexual release, but let's reduce these to one evolution-based reason: we get horny when we're compelled to create alongside someone or something that's not ourselves. We feel horny as evolution's encouragement for us to enjoy doing so.

A desire for co-creation → a desire to mate ourselves with another.

The more that desire is related to the use of our bodies to deeply register that co-creative process, and the more that desire is driven by your biology itself (rather than your trained mind), the more likely that desire will become sexual.

A desire for co-creation driven by the body → a desire to sexually mate ourselves with another

Sometimes the others we're thinking of aren't people, but broad situations. That is, we may want to co-create, but the *kind* of co-creative partner our body has in mind might be as important as the co-creative experience itself.

A body-driven desire for the co-creation experience (with or without another body) → a desire for sexual experience (with or without another body)

So ages of people have found that it may be easier, simpler, or more enjoyable to pleasure *themselves* than to go through the trouble of getting a partner to do it. This is especially true when your partner options prefer to shame you for going outside of their various rule sets. *My body wants release and would prefer it with you, but you hound me. I'd rather just get the release myself and be done with it.* The chain of emotions and wants that describes my transition from slightly stimulated to full blast horny is the story of my Dimension 4. Unlike several of the other dimensions, the makeup of this Dimension 4 chain changes all the time, though there are some generic observations we can make about it.

Knowing what turns you on at the highest level helps you discover your "base of operations" for your most contented relationship.

It is so important to spell this out in terms of forms, though. Body parts disappear when the lights go off, but our evolved interactions with them remain. If you like big tits, then a place of partner-sponsored *nurturance* may be part of the space from which you build your best partner experiences. If you like German men, then the cold, controlled, handsomeness that distinguishes the German archetype may suggest *cold, controlled, situational command* as your base of operations. I like sleepy eyes, so *mellow, dreamy, smoothness* provides a good context for my best relationships.

This book was prompted by two critical events in my life that occurred immediately prior. One of them I'll tell you about in a later chapter, the other one was as follows:

> Every year and a half or so I enter a new phase in what I like sexually. My most recent phase drew me to Iranian women. It came out of nowhere, and had no prompt I could think of. The more I investigated this preference compared to my previous phases, the more important this latest phase became. I've been taught that Iran has been a kind of anti-Western culture for as long as I've been alive. Certainly there is some truth in this since the 1979 revolution, but there is also more to it. As a country-form, Iran is one of the few cultures which, broadly, loudly defies the basic Westernisms of selfishness, transactionalism, and inhumility. That is, my subconscious sees Iran as taking a values stand that many other places agree with, but are not poised to openly air. And even though the country has FAR more problems (of all kinds) than we do here in the US, the politics wasn't the point. Once I got tired enough of accepting my training in the kinds of self-aggrandizing things I talked about in Dimension 6, I decided to write this book. America is full of great things, including a tolerance for books like this. I still think that our openness to amplifying individuals' dreams is second to none. But we have an unhappiness that can't be easily corrected from within—a form of social and civic disempowerment, a self-divisiveness which frustrates us psychologically, and makes us unable to find happiness past a certain point because "that party over there" or "those people over yonder" couldn't possibly offer anything worthwhile. The

Iranian state, though not one I'd live under, is one that stands on a singularly determined, vocalized Rule Set that we wouldn't want to match, but which we still need pieces of— just like the activities earlier in this chapter. So when my sexual interest changed, it was actually my expressive context which changed. Combined with some averaged body features that appeal to me, the Iranian woman marked a decision to finally write outside of the transactional world we know here. For their own self-development, I'd encourage readers to try a shift in preference like this. It's not really about the sex. It's about the figurative studio in which you make your art. The things that turn you on are like the furniture you'll decorate your creative studio with. It pays to go shopping outside of your own house.

Surprise! The things that turn you on may not come in the form of those things

So you like tall men. But this one is short. Thanks to *Sex in 12* so far, you're sure that tall men are the only way to go and that's it. Wrong. Tallness is a physical announcement, not a behavioral actuality. Even if it is one of your "must be big" qualities from Dimension 9, the Dimension 9 qualities were still intended to reflect your broadcast wishes which can change forms depending on who your preferred audience is. Sure your friends may be awed by your tall man's tallness as a feature of your world. But they might also be awed by you and your man's tall *business enterprise* regardless of what his bodily height is. Same "type" of announcement effect, different lifestyle patterns for you. My Iranian woman may in fact be an American blonde who's also tired of the inhumility. Your outgoing girlfriend may in fact be two guys who also anchor the network of other guys' attention. Mary's rich beau may actually be a beloved, welcome-anywhere middle classer with even more of the social mobility that riches typically buy. It's good to know the form, but restrictive to ignore the form's broader effects. Forms that don't look like themselves can change you forever as soon as you realize you like them. They may expose you to spaces you never thought could be so good. But you have to drop the judgment and accept the gifts where they are given. Say I love you.

Say I'm Sorry

It's often the case that when we talk about the value in things we let slip by, we're confronted with how wrong we were in hindsight. We may be trained to say things like *Oh well, what's done is done* or *Can't change the past* or *They played their part in it too!* It may not occur to us to own up to our part, because we may think of doing so as inviting a guilty verdict that we don't deserve. To make matters worse, sometimes we try to own up to our part—perhaps apologizing to the Other—only to find that they won't own up to theirs. Or maybe they twist the knife saying, "Damn straight you were wrong." Maybe they belabor the conflict when really you both need to just move on.

But here we are. We've looked at the forms we prefer and we realize that we threw something away that perhaps we shouldn't have (had we known better at the time). We know we were wrong to judge them, to embarrass them, to treat them as less, then kick them out. We can't go back to them, for even if they forgave us, there are simply too many corpses on that battlefield. No one wants to go back there. The disappointment one might feel in realizations like this can border on guilt, but we know that guilt really is no good. What do we do? We say I'm sorry. But not necessarily to anyone in particular—preferably not for any reason in particular. Instead, we say I'm sorry as a general act of humility towards our better selves, and as a way of opening a commitment to our better selves to make more beneficial choices next time. Let me give you an example.

> The relationship I described earlier, the one with the "bad person," ended on a terrible note. In a later communication with her which I couldn't avoid, her approach to me was as poisonous as it had ever been. But I had forgiven her the day we ended it, had tried to ask for what I needed politely, but when it didn't come, more battling ensued. And that's where we've left off to this day. The thing is though, even though my

exchange with her was by far the worst one I have ever experienced in my life, choosing her to begin with was also one of the best decisions I ever made. She's beautiful, she's fiery, she commands many. She tries her best where no one else would, and regardless of my history with her as a person, I still respect her bravery as a determined will. She carries a lot of burdens and I know it. In hindsight, I threw her away because, together, we lacked the tools to be better people to each other. More than anything, I know that—had I known more about those invisible assumptions we were working with—I would have tried harder to use them effectively. And I'm sorry. Not for—or to—either of us, but because given the tools I have now, I know I wouldn't let another relationship go the way that one went. It's not regret; we both did the best we knew at the time. And it's not guilt; without better communication our temperaments just don't favor an easier dynamic. My "I'm sorry" is just an acknowledgement *to my better self* that I'll do my best, going forward, with what I now know. It's a commitment to the present—not an indictment of the past or a burden for the future—to honor the fire she brought into my life where no one else has had greater nerve. And I respect that.

There are countless ways to misunderstand someone, and countless points on the timeline where it's possible to fall off track. You can apologize to the Other for Monday's fight, but you might still have had it on Tuesday. When it comes to Dimension 4, being sorry for "something" only limits the reach of your reversal, and lets your other crimes in the chain go unaddressed. "I'm sorry you misunderstood" is the asshole's way of reassigning blame once again. "I'm sorry I hurt you" is genuine, but in deep Self-Water, limited. It also reinforces your own power to "hurt." It also attaches (billboard-style) the hurt to the apology. Without apologizing for anything in particular, a general and sincere I'm sorry allows us to address the whole chain of events that led us here, and people who try both versions will see the difference.

There's the broad *I'm sorry* and there's the specific *I'm sorry for...* Semantically alone, the first version is easier for moving on.

When you're ready to do better for yourself going forward, *I'm sorry* followed by 1) the things you'll do better or 2) the messages you'll listen to for doing better is good enough. You don't need to feel regret, you don't need to admit being wrong if you don't think you were wrong, you don't need to qualify it or belabor the issue. All you're doing is acknowledging that the way it was wasn't cool compared to the way you intend it to be going forward. This whole process is one type of forgiveness.

Fantasies as They Are

Fantasies often involve scenarios full of symbols and can be interpreted in ways similar to dreams. If you fantasize about living in a mansion then that mansion's forms reflect your temporary base of operations for creating what you create. If you fantasize about winning the lottery then access to social mobility through a surprise burst of reward may be what you'd prefer to build your creative works upon at the moment. And then of course there are the good ole' carnal fantasies. If you're a girl who dreams of doing your guy from behind, then a kind of power reversal may be your thing at the moment—bedroom or not. If you're a guy who dreams that your girl is giving head to another guy, third person enjoyment of your dynamic may be what you're after. We'll see much more of this in the next two chapters. Just know that whatever turns you on in symbols shows the space you feel like being in for that moment's creative agenda.

So why did we talk so much about "I'm sorry" and your biases and all that? Because your fantasies and your Dimension 4 can only go as far as your biases and your guilt-proneness will allow them to go. I've met a woman or two who's whole story rendered them bisexual, but they were in such denial that they terrorized themselves and everyone else with their self-destruction. I've met a couple of transgender people who had such a rough time working out their own transitions that they struggled to develop safe psychological spaces for seeking fulfillment.

If biases and guilt follow you around, your fantasy world will stay stuck in advertised models. The standard co-creation we're shown has nowhere near the depth of expressive potential that you can pull off in minutes, but it has to be okay for you to exit your mind's jail first. Try it and you'll see what I mean. No one can love more deeply than the person who loves *everything* within himself—past crimes also considered.

Dimension 4 Sex

Dimension 4 sex relies on what you want to feel at the moment. In order to do it well, you'll need to follow your intuitive sense of what you want to experience next. This process is challenging to really pull off without a dose of Dimension 3 or Dimension 1 instinct, but you can at least ride the emotional ship to a proper destination.

So much of Dimension 4 requires that you put yourself in the right mood-settings ahead of time, so that the contents of your fantasies may be better directed through subconscious input. Those of us who've ever banged in an awkward place know that it's not nearly as fun as the porn flicks make it seem, and has surprisingly minimal appeal in most people's sexual history. Because our fantasies often entail the fantastic, it's *very* easy for us to be limited to only their most basic components. Still, you can help give more life to your Self-Water by positioning yourself in a place where all is possible—including the targets of your bias, the operations base for your self-efficacy, and the past forms you failed to give credence. Make efforts in your waking world to address these things and you'll discover the value in contexts previously locked to you. Once unlocked you'll find out something that many of us have found as we've become more open to practices beyond our training: You have no idea what feeling is until you've let yourself feel it all over your soul. A person freed from psychological blockages is a person with all of life's toys at her command.

Remember:

- For good Dimension 4 sex, put yourself in mental and physical spaces most conducive to the richest fantasies. A lot of these spaces will be related to the packages of experiences represented by things in previous fantasies you've had.
- It doesn't pay to hold onto psychological baggage. Even your richest desires can sometimes be only big fish in your closed little pond. If you want your fantasies to be off the hook, you'll need for the frameworks available to you to be the same. Things you hate, things you judge, and pasts that bother you will all hold critical pieces of your imagination hostage. They will also limit the sources from which you can experience certain more exotic forms of love and pleasure. Try to clear this stuff out if you can, or else expect your Dimension 4 persona to remain forever stuck as one the biggest underachievers in your psychological repertoire.

13 (PART 1) DIMENSION 10: *Sex Under Limits*

Let me share with you the other story of an event that changed my life, and prompted the writing of this book:

> Every once in a while, I'll visit a porn site to see what's out there. People may not believe this, but I visit mainly for insight into the patterns I observe—how people titillate, how they seduce, what constitutes the difference between beauty, allure, hotness and sexiness, and how all of these have different feelings that they trigger when you observe them. To this day I remain intrigued by how the standards of beauty in America have changed so drastically in two decades—from sophisticated career blonde to sassy, witty brunette—and how even porn has evolved more of a comic, gee whiz flair than the old swanky seduction scenarios. It's true that the porn industry is ahead of everybody else. It's that field that taps into people's desires long before they

become acceptable in the mainstream, mocking yet predicting the latest nasty desires secretly churning within the collective unconscious, and turning that satire upon our norms into dollars.

While *Sex in 12* was still just a twinkle in my eye, I found myself on the porn site looking for Czech women in order to learn more about why I liked them so much. But I didn't find any that appealed to me. Instead I noticed how the pictures were even less interesting than usual (I haven't been stimulated very much by porn in years), and started noticing how some of the pics were actually a little annoying. *MORE selfies, huh? *Sigh*...Let's look for some mature milfs instead.* I swear this is how porn directors must feel after a while. You really *can* see too much ass in one lifetime. Anyway, the milfs (mother I'd love to fuck; a.k.a. "older" women) looked like they were about 30. *What!? That ain't no milf! She could be my daughter!* So I searched for "Matures" and got 40 and 50 year-olds. *Okay. But I'm 38 and these still look young to me.* So I searched for "Old and hot." 30 and 40 year-olds again. Finally, I unleashed the ultimate search term: "Grannies." 60s and 70s were the result. *Bingo.* Now let me tell you what I observed.

I like women of all ages, but there's something that changes as you move up in age. Although I was not as hot-stimulated by the older pics, I was noticeably more emotion-stimulated. It would amount to the difference between Dimension 1 and Dimension 12. Younger women were much more likely to advertise their youth and slam the camera with attitude. Older women were more likely to show their assets and convey to you the sense of pleasure they still felt with themselves. Big boned grannies, grannies with giant telescope glasses, older women with wrinkled skin and the freckles of age...I wasn't hot-stimulated, but there was something that many of them had which was <u>honestly</u> more satisfying to look at than many of the air-brushed young things I had seen minutes prior. What was that something? I'd say it was a security with themselves. It showed in the genuinely self-possessed or joy-inviting faces they wore instead of that ego-slinging pucker of the standard hot girl. There were fewer posed contortions made to fire boobage like missiles across the camera, and more of a survey of bodily grandeur upon which the eye might carefully wander. In terms of ratios, the number of truly beautiful women among the matures, milfs, and grannies was about the same or higher compared to the number you'd count among the younger hot things. As usual, you'd find fewer true beauties in the porn space than sexy women, fewer sexy women than hot women, fewer hot women than alluring women, and fewer alluring women than simply sexualized ones—the latter of which far and away dominate the porn space.

And I found myself smiling a lot more while viewing the older pictures. *You go you 75-year-old! Rock that package you got!* One older lady let it all hang out with her de-perkied business confidently put in front of thousands of eyes—thick rimmed bifocals and all. I kept looking and I kept wondering why so much of what I was seeing was so satisfying. That is, until I finally figured it out: It's not the forced turn-on, the selfie strut, or the makeup that compels a person to keep staring at you harmoniously as he stares at you—free of forced tension but easily in his absorption of you. It's not the flawless skin or the hiding of lines. Beyond all that, there is an overall persona that one sends through the camera that makes it obvious to all that you need no disguises to fully believe in the value you hold; you enjoy this body and everyone else should enjoy it too. And, if you're convinced enough to tell it to the world, then even decades of life won't be able to hide it. A superficial observer might miss it, but those of us who know your true value can see through to the soul.

There is some myth out there that older people don't fuck. As usual, this is because people advanced in age in our society are advertised into silence, drowned out by the noisy blockbuster of 20-something youth. We associate youth with passion and virility. We associate age with being worn out and depleted of attractiveness. What my trip into the world of grannies taught me, however, is that things don't cease to ignite passion just because they age; viewers don't need to be made maddeningly horny by you in order for you to be considered beautiful; there are definitely forms of beauty that you gain more of the closer you get to certain among Life's limits; being able to operate within those age, disability, and other expressive limits give you a unique and undying resilience that weaker expressers will never possess. In that aesthetic resilience lies one of the key components of beauty. Let's redefine beauty now.

> I knew two women who were friends years ago, one hot, one pretty. The hot one attracted all kinds of men while the pretty one attracted many men and a lot of respect. As the years went on, it was clear that the pretty one had a sophisticated self-possession which drove her to create many new things in the world from within. And the hot one stayed hot amongst a sea of other hot, sometimes hotter ones. By most standards, you might have thought that having more of a certain socially desirable trait set you up to go farther in the world. It does kind of, but only to the point that there are more people willing to promote you partly on the basis of that trait. Beyond the point where that trait stops working on people who hold the opportunities, no flawless figure will teach you how to be influencer of the systems you're still subject to, and though you may have a kingdom full of fans, the self-possessed people who own you will make a greater mark on their worlds than just another social image. This isn't a criticism of attractive people—only an observation that, without offerings that genuinely come from self-possession, attractive people have a habit of blending into each other. Today, the "merely" pretty and sophisticated woman I knew

stands alone in her dream, and the hot one vanished into who knows where.

We celebrate excessive passion in our relationships and in our politics, placing a premium on what I think of as "allure" in contrast to true beauty. **Allure keeps you staring even if you don't want to**; beauty keeps you staring because your process of staring likes itself. Allure lures eyes under the allurer's power; beauty keeps the eyes under the eyer's engagement. Because it relies on the allurer's power, allure's effect on the viewer goes away when the allurer does. But beauty relies on its viewer's appreciation, so beauty endures even after its object disappears.

In our society many people strive for beauty but can only manage **hotness—where people accept you've convincingly passed the standard of socialized allure whether or not they themselves are attracted by you**. Still others are said to be beautiful but are really only **sexy—alluring in a way that elicits the drive for co-creative action in a viewer**. Many men and women who don't enter that arena—but who still have appearances which draw viewer's a harmonious appreciation of their sex-typical look—are called **good looking** and **pretty** respectively, where these describe how a general person's experience of your presence meets the standards of socialized sex-typical company even if the viewer isn't specifically attracted to you. And **beauty** is the experience where the viewer wishes to continue viewing harmoniously in the way that he views. ***All things can be beautiful if only they would engage the things that love viewing them.*** But the more a person believes he or she <u>needs</u> to add other things to their image in order to bring out their attractiveness—more poses, more dress up, more makeup, and so on—the harder it is to see their own beauty behind the extras so commonly employed by others. Nice clothes and makeup are great and can surely make you beautiful in one way, but until we're allowed to see you at your "normal" and get the chance to view you harmoniously in that way, it's hard to know how much of that beauty is yours and how much of it belongs to the makeup. The situation I described at the beginning of this chapter offered me more opportunities to view this second kind of beauty. The feeling you got as a viewer was unique to every woman you looked at—something that can't as often be said with hotness of the prepackaged kind. Spill the wine.

An Introduction to Dimension 10

Although we sometimes like to think of sex in terms of limitlessness, clearly there are boundaries all over the subject. We don't like to injure people, we prefer not to make them too uncomfortable if we can help it, we respect certain privacy constraints and other preferences, and we like to keep in mind that people prefer to hear or not hear certain things while we're at it. All of these place limits on our bedroom behavior. Outside of the bedroom there are even more limits actively imposing themselves upon us at any time. Up to now we've spent a lot of time focusing on the type of sex that *enables* certain options. Now we'll talk about the kinds of sex which relies heavily on *disabling* options. This kind of sex is really fun for those who get it, I tell you, and for me ultimately marked the central turning point between my regular discontented partnership life and the all-good life thereafter. If you're going to encounter limits in your relationships (and we all will) one of the best things you can do is script them by your own hand. **Dimension 10** holds as its central feature the design on **sex under specifically chosen limits**, bringing us into the world of age, disability, fetishes, and all the other factors which wall us in...

(...or perhaps awaken our approach to control?)

We began with a discussion of age and beauty in order to illustrate a key point. You are beautiful wherever some party can't stop experiencing who you are with that harmonious feeling of theirs. Physical beauty is only a part of the story. Your actions, your communication and—heavily increasingly as you age—*the impressions you leave* on a room are the other components of your beauty. Beauty is a kind of attractiveness, but not all brands of attractiveness are the same. Society is full of people going out their way to be attractive, but even where people achieve this, popular attractiveness shared with a sea of other popularly attractive people isn't necessarily related to your beauty. I'm sure you've seen plenty of people who were attractive but not beautiful, plenty of red-carpet moments that came and went, dresses and suits that endured longer than our memory of their wearers did. Where beauty and allure are present in the same person, the allure will continue to affect viewers more strongly until the allurer stops luring, giving the viewer a chance to choose with his own eyes instead. One of the main benefits of age is that more viewers have this chance with you, so the likelihood that your relationships will be of higher quality goes up noticeably.

My guardians say that "personal beauty is a form intended to advance one with easier social ease. Especially for those who aren't born into privileged classes, beauty is essential to mobility." So we don't want to hate on beautiful people (or, relatedly, rich people) because the whole point of that *is* to get you promoted faster by others. BUT, in that promotion there is a price. We can consider beauty to be a kind of social "speed" among people who desire, while riches are a kind of social "reach" among people who access opportunities. As with traditional speed, the average contact with the thing you pass is lower so that solidly enduring relationships and the validated value that comes with it is harder to come by until you get to the finish line. Beautiful people overall have an easier time trusting and bonding with their final group of peers who share their social tier, but fewer people above or below that tier. Riches is similar in that longer reach prevents people outside of your tier of access from getting close, and like being tall this can cause problems with you being treated like a commodity rather than being seen for gifts that are truly yours. Most people who are not rich may find it hard to believe that rich people have any problems, but they do. When you're rich you worry about bigger versions of things which should, on principle, be simple. You're more likely to protect things that fall into your circumference which really don't deserve to be protected. These could be objects or people. Most of all, when you're rich, you're more likely to put up with more and more complicated kinds of disrespect, treachery, and other subpar exchanges simply because the circles of people who hand you this kind of thing are more likely to overlap with yours in ways that you can't easily repair. Accordingly, what the rich have in reach, the poor have in power to self-express (as opposed to expression constrained by social expectation). What the beautiful have in social mobility, the normal have in solid and trustable belonging. These are the limits of status. As we seek to move past where we are, the things we pass up very often must be abandoned completely.

1. It's rare to see a rich person lead a revolution, no matter how much they care personally. There's too much to lose; the people on such tiers don't need to care; and the people below those tiers usually aren't informed enough to make use of the tools which the status-bearing person has.
2. So we can imagine that many a duke and governor may have really wanted to make changes to their kingdom, only to get tied up in battles with other governors.
3. Meanwhile the peasants and poor, because they knew no such restraints, were free to riot at will.
4. Even those high in status must live within the limits of their tied hands.
5. Those low in status live under the threat of being smacked by their creditors.
6. The beautiful are a beacon burning in the eyes of the desirous,
   7. and they are often constrained to trade intimacies only among their own kind.
8. The normal are braced by their friends, but blind to the opportunities their masters hold access to.
9. The sick must wean their nurturance from healthy sources,
   10. or take medicines to repair them.
11. The healthy are challenged to keep that health through stretched physical feats,
   12. or lose that health to inflexibility, limited to being serviced in their shells by those who'll need to reach places they can't reach.

13. While intellectuals know causality, they also know high nerves.
14. Non-intellectuals or anti-intellectuals know only what they can see and taste.
15. Men are confined to standards of manhood.
16. Women are confined to standards of womanhood.
17. And each is unable to be the other.
18. Each is pressured to maintain their body-typical appearance, or else lose their masculinity or femininity.
19. Both must remain in the world of reality where neither pretended
    20. nor actual non-reality are thought acceptable.
21. Finally, the strange thing about being human is that we can't feel our own bodies, even though our bodies do feel.
22. We must age and die.
23. We must form relationships and commit to them, but not outside the rules of each kind.
24. And we are required to play roles so that our worth can be realized.
25. We're typically expected to be committed to someone at some point, but once that happens we can usually
    26. no longer enjoy commitment-like relationships
    27. from other partner-like people.
28. And in our committed relationship, the standard escalator from liking through sex and some kind of referenceable love forms a template that we're often punished for straying from
29. Our bodies are ours, but meant to be seen by others.
30. Our bodies are subject to certain appearances and subject to certain prejudices,
    31. so that the number and kinds of connections we form are restricted.
32. Our connections depend on what we want to create in life, but we're pressured to create in the stereotypical male and female ways.
33. If we have power, we'll almost always have people we're responsible for.

34. If we have solid belonging, we'll almost always have people responsible for us.
35. And if we ever ask other to use us as *their* canvas we may experience this life from an entirely new perspective, but people stuck in the normal perspective will almost certainly not understand.

These are some of the limits that are common to us. Now, before you turn the page, get something to write with.

Take a couple of minutes to go back over the above list and

- Put an × next to any of the items that bother you, or which constitutes a fact you are continually, negatively reminded of.
- Put a ✓ next to any of the items that you like or really appreciate in your experience.
- Leave unmarked any items that don't matter.

Below are a mere few of the physical practices and tools which approximate the previous limits.

1. It's rare to see a rich person lead a revolution, no matter how much they care personally. There's too much to lose; the people on such tiers don't need to care; and the people below those tiers usually aren't informed enough to make use of the tools which the status-bearing person has. **Sex toys, Smoking** (for those simulating the rich and sophisticated in power).

2. So we can imagine that many a duke and governor may have really wanted to make changes to their kingdom, only to get tied up in battles with other governors. **Stocks, Tied to the bed**

3. Meanwhile the peasants and poor, because they knew no such restraints, were free to riot at will. **Hard sex, throat fucking, dildoing.**

4. Even those high in status must live within the limits of their tied hands. **Bondage**

5. Those low in status live under the threat of being smacked by their creditors. **Spanking, Flogging**

6. The beautiful are a beacon burning in the eyes of the desirous, **Candle play**

7. And they are often constrained to trade intimacies only among their own kind. **Partner Swapping**

8. The normal are braced by their friends, but blind to the opportunities their masters hold access to. **Blindfolding**

9. The sick must wean their nurturance from healthy sources, **Assorted oral**

10. or take medicines to repair them. **Alcohol, psychedelics, and other substances**

11. The healthy are challenged to keep that health through stretched physical feats, **Kama Sutra, 69, Doggystyle, and other Novel Sexual Positions, Certain Yoga**

12. or lose that health to inflexibility, limited to being serviced in their shells by those who'll need to reach places they can't reach. **Body Worship, Stillness**
13. While intellectuals know causality, they also know high nerves. **Vibrators and Other Sex Machines, ASMR, Tickling, Feather Play, Sex Stories** (collectively: "Frequency Play")
14. Non-intellectuals or anti-intellectuals know only what they can see and taste. **Edibles, Porn Flicks and Images, Body Play**
15. Men are confined to standards of manhood. **Ball cage**
16. Women are confined to standards of womanhood. **Chastity belt, corset**
17. And each is unable to be the other. **Penis needling, Strap on, Shemale**
18. Each is pressured to maintain their body-typical appearance, or else lose their masculinity or femininity. **Shaving (normal or ritualized)**
19. Both must remain in the world of reality where neither pretended **Kigurumi**
    20. nor actual non-reality are thought acceptable. **Games, Hentai**
21. Finally, the strange thing about being human is that we can't feel our own bodies, even though our bodies do feel. **Latex, Fishnet, Lingerie, Boots and other Wearables**
22. We must age and die. **Mature, MILF, Teen, Necro**
23. We must form relationships and commit to them, but not outside the rules of each kind. **Step-brother & sister, Daddy & Baby Girl, Boss's Wife, Side Dick & Mistress, Laughing & Crying and other Emotion-Substitution Play**
24. And we are required to play roles so that our worth can be realized. **Pretend Strangers, Maid, Striptease & General Role Play**
25. We're typically expected to be committed to someone at some point, but once that happens we can usually **Friends with Benefits / Fuck Buddy**
    26. no longer enjoy commitment-like relationships **Polyamory**

27. from other partner-like people. **Swinging**
28. And in our committed relationship, the standard escalator from liking through sex and some kind of referenceable love forms a template that we're often punished for straying from **Open Relationship**
29. Our bodies are ours, but meant to be seen by others. **Exhibitionism, Public Sex, Size Queen, Hot-partner and other [Dimension 9] broadcastables**
30. Our bodies are subject to certain appearances and subject to certain prejudices, **Attraction to a Specific Nationality or Body Type**
    31. so that the number and kinds of connections we form are restricted. **Group Sex, Cuddle Party**
32. Our connections depend on what we want to create in life, but we're pressured to create in the stereotypical male and female ways. **Tantric Sex, Male Internal Orgasm, Female Squirting**
33. If we have power, we'll almost always have people we're responsible for. **Dom, Master**
34. If we have solid belonging, we'll almost always have people responsible for us. **sub, slave**
35. And if we ever ask other to use us as *their* canvas we may experience this life from an entirely new perspective, but people stuck in the normal perspective will almost certainly not understand. **Creampie, Bukkake, Pissing, Body Paint**

Have your partner do this same exercise, using the blank list below, Putting a ✓ or × next to statements they resonate with or statements that bother them respectively. Every other statement should be left blank.

1. It's rare to see a rich person lead a revolution, no matter how much they care personally. There's too much to lose; the people on such tiers don't need to care; and the people below those tiers usually aren't informed enough to make use of the tools which the status-bearing person has.
2. So we can imagine that many a duke and governor may have really wanted to make changes to their kingdom, only to get tied up in battles with other governors.
3. Meanwhile the peasants and poor, because they knew no such restraints, were free to riot at will.
4. Even those high in status must live within the limits of their tied hands.
5. Those low in status live under the threat of being smacked by their creditors.
6. The beautiful are a beacon burning in the eyes of the desirous,
   7. and they are often constrained to trade intimacies only among their own kind.
8. The normal are braced by their friends, but blind to the opportunities their masters hold access to.
9. The sick must wean their nurturance from healthy sources,
   10. or take medicines to repair them.
11. The healthy are challenged to keep that health through stretched physical feats,
   12. or lose that health to inflexibility, limited to being serviced in their shells by those who'll need to reach places they can't reach.
13. While intellectuals know causality, they also know high nerves.
14. Non-intellectuals or anti-intellectuals know only what they can see and taste.
15. Men are confined to standards of manhood.
16. Women are confined to standards of womanhood.
17. And each is unable to be the other.
18. Each is pressured to maintain their body-typical appearance, or else lose their masculinity or femininity.

19. Both must remain in the world of reality where neither pretended

    20. nor actual non-reality are thought acceptable.

21. Finally, the strange thing about being human is that we can't feel our own bodies, even though our bodies do feel.

22. We must age and die.

23. We must form relationships and commit to them, but not outside the rules of each kind.

24. And we are required to play roles so that our worth can be realized.

25. We're typically expected to be committed to someone at some point, but once that happens we can usually

    26. no longer enjoy commitment-like relationships

    27. from other partner-like people.

28. And in our committed relationship, the standard escalator from liking through sex and some kind of referenceable love forms a template that we're often punished for straying from

29. Our bodies are ours, but meant to be seen by others.

30. Our bodies are subject to certain appearances and subject to certain prejudices,

    31. so that the number and kinds of connections we form are restricted.

32. Our connections depend on what we want to create in life, but we're pressured to create in the stereotypical male and female ways.

33. If we have power, we'll almost always have people we're responsible for.

34. If we have solid belonging, we'll almost always have people responsible for us.

35. And if we ever ask other to use us as *their* canvas we may experience this life from an entirely new perspective, but people stuck in the normal perspective will almost certainly not understand.

Look at anything they put a ✓ or ✗ next to that also has your ✓ or ✗ next to it.

If you're down, try it out.

After producing the fetish inventory, I asked the guardians to give me some input. Here's what they said:

You've really made quite a list there OML. By all rights the human repertoire of options for expressing towards each other is impressive indeed. It is far more varied than the options available to the plants and animals, for example. But there is an unfortunate problem. Although you have constructed this list, many people who are new to the world it describes will be too busy gawking at it to understand its implications. The point is, where humans normally play out pretend scenarios in their waking lives, pretending that an angry boss is meaningful, pretending that a birthday gift indicates something more than an obligated purchase, pretending that things like dates are substitutes for genuinely felt emotions at a distance, many humans will continue to swap reality for fantasy to their detriment.

So many burdens that a human carries are unnecessary; you carry them because your friends do not consider your life to be real if you refuse. Not only do you carry these burdens, but you carry the additional burden of disallowing questioning of those burdens. So you are not typically allowed to ask whether earning money for work is important. And you are not allowed to ask whether having intercourse with your best friend's wife is wrong if everyone gives permission. Obviously we are not here to change how you all work, but we want you to understand that people who live in confined frameworks within confined frameworks will likely not see this list as an opportunity to try new things with their loved ones. They will only see it as an occasion for giggling. The idea that giggling over this actually makes them good candidates for feather play or certain kinds of "ASMR" will be lost to them. Some people just won't see it.

But we are confident that the die has been cast. When a human thinks of the limits that confine his life, he has several options: to accept those limits, to deny those limits, to own those limits, or to distract himself. As you can imagine, the last choice is the one which most people have been trained to embrace, but increasingly there is work in the liberation efforts of humanity which make the third choice a much more popular one. More people are realizing that, when a messenger presents them with an option to free themselves, they should at least consider it if the alternative would only be a return to the status quo. The challenge for you will be not so much convincing readers that these are options, but in explaining to people where to find others who will also enjoy these options in the readers' company. It is better that we explain this part for you, because the general lay of the land—despite the existence of many more liberal groups in these matters—is still very hostile in almost all societies all around the world. The grounding in male and female biologies runs everywhere in every direction, and until humans come to see equality in this particular area, liberated relationships as a mainstream topic will remain difficult to achieve. Furthermore, in answer to the question of where one can find such people in his community, it is no secret in major cities that such groups are there, but the cost (as you have seen yourself) is that those groups are often so defined by the sexual aspects of the relationships that issues of their own psychological need or unresolved developmental issues often get neglected.

It is much healthier to simply find a close friend with whom a person can talk about such things and present them with ideas. Historically you have noticed that in this conservative city of yours (San Antonio, TX, US) people tend to see an open discussion of sexuality, love, or tenderness as a request for sex. Automatically, some societies are trained to demonize those who even use the word in the company of an attached person. This will not change for a while here, but still there are some who are not so closed. There are places in your land which are more open, but also not so capable of sending apparently sane messages to the rest of the land, such that the revolution you seek, though successful, must start in some country other than the United States. The pride runs too deep here. Readers who are interested in capitalizing on the knowledge of themselves would do better to investigate countries like Switzerland and the UAE, whose focus on globalism transcends any interest in *closing* national borders. To liberate their people psychologically, a society must educate its people to think globally. Germany is also better at this than most, though still very conservative. Your readers need not do anything with this knowledge or what we are telling them. They need only supplement the knowledge in this chapter with the following point: To surround oneself with liberated thinkers, one must breathe in the energy of a liberated society. Not a liberal society. Not a liberty society. But a liber*ated* society. The US is not liberated. Few lands are. Those that are, like New Zealand—high in community and social capital—are seldom listened to because of the practicalities of economics. The world under Western hegemony does not really listen to any nation in terms other than the economic or the military. Accordingly, educational marvels like Finland, Sweden, or Singapore—innovators like Japan or South Korea and forward attempters like Brasilia, are not elevated highly enough in the rest of the World's consciousness even though the rest of the world very much needs what these places have to offer.

You asked a moment ago whether you should move this rather long note to an appendix. You can, but it would be better where it is. We know that a discussion of globalism does not seem very appropriate in a chapter on human proclivities under restriction, but the business of Saturn is not to titillate. It is to bind. Readers should know that what you have written should be taken seriously enough to be placed in a global context in the same way that your country's last few Presidents have been elected on the basis of charisma. People's sense of what makes a good relationship has implications for who they think constitutes a good person. Who they think constitutes a good person has implications for who they think constitutes a good leader. In a society where the exemplars are praised for how much they can acquire, the emphasis is on knowing no limits, and that is not good for you. Limits are everywhere and should be embraced by those willing and able to take responsibility for others, and our guess is that the leaders among your readers will be more likely to see this, more likely to try what it says, and more likely to adopt psychologically liberated relationships decades before others do. It's all in time.

To attract fellow limiters, it is better to find a friend with whom you can discuss these things. The conversation goes something like this: I read that limits reflect fetishes and fetishes reflect self-determination against what we were taught. What do you think? If the reply is, Fetishes are nasty, then you know the person wasn't listening to the self-determination part. If the reply is, Limits, what do you mean? Then you are more likely dealing with a mind that won't let itself get past the starting gate. They may not criticize you the way the first person would, but they might also require that you walk them through every single step of the logic. There will be a time when minds like this will have their curriculum, but the leaders have too much work to bother with that now. Instead, if the third reply applies, Self-determination? Let's talk some more, then you can go from there. This test is simple enough to weed out like minds from those not ready, but we want you to know that you will encounter quite a few judges if you do this incorrectly. Men should generally avoid this test and let the actions invite the subject instead. But women can use the test. For men, the challenge is to have faith and discipline, shunning the "pick-up line" quality of it. A stubborn enough woman will eat him alive for it, even if he honestly wants to know. With a heart in the right place, a man can attract a like-minded woman who understands this by showing that he understands her, and that it is not his priority to bed her in special ways. He must correct his mis-trained animal desires against the current American emasculating society, recover his ability to define his preferences without some woman dictating it from afar, and let his newfound focus provide him with the partner he seeks. Pick-up lines or topics which sound like them are not the answer for him.

You've written all that we have to tell you. Let's close this chapter with one final paragraph. Namaste.

Conclusion

It seems we didn't talk much about the details of Dimension 10. But this dimension is so distinct and your choice to approach it so straightforward that I suppose there isn't much more to say. If you're okay with limits and want to own the ones that follow you around, Dimension 10's structuring practices are available for you to survey. You can go all the way to the Kasbah if you have the right partner, but finding one will definitely be a matter of resolve on your part. While most of us probably learned of Limit-Sex as consisting of that nasty space where the nymphos go, it's really nothing more than a more diversified version of the lingerie, sexy music, stripteasing, wine-drinking couple's night that we've surely already accepted. Baby steps through blindfolds and candles is what I say. Whatever you decide, you'll need a partner you trust in order to enter much of this territory, though there are certainly things you can do on your own. Sex under limits may not appeal to people who would prefer not to look at any limits at all, but for those people who do, there will be few further rules that can hold them beyond the world full of those they write for themselves.

What follows is a different Chapter 13 from a different book that I don't plan to publish, but which fits the previous discussion of "structure" nicely. I've included it right here in its original form as a kind of exercise that you may find informative as you explore the rest of the content of this *S12*.

13 (PART 2) SEXUALITIES

So many times I've found myself explaining different sexuality dimensions to others. I know you know about them, but I'm summarizing them in a table for reference.

Component	What It's Called		
Seeking a certain number of mates for forming stable relationships	**Number**		
	Category		**Its Opposite**
	Monogamous (mono): one mate		**Strict Polyamorous** (s-poly): number of mates is not one
	Celibate (single): no mates		**Polyamorous** (poly): one or more mates
Seeking same-sex or opposite-sex mates	**Gender**		
	Category		**Its Opposite**
	Heterosexual (hetero): opposite sex preferred		**Homosexual** (gay or lesbian): same sex preferred
	Bisexual (bi): both sexes preferred		**Asexual**: neither sexes preferred
Seeking (broadly) more dominant or submissive interaction styles in mates	**Polarity Preference**		
	Category		**Its Opposite**
	Alpha: submissive seeking		**Beta**: dominant seeking
	Neutral: interaction polarity doesn't matter		
Preferring to interact with others using a more male-trained or female-trained style	**Polarity**		
	Masculinity	These don't have opposites, but exist on a hormonal scale in everyone's biology	
	Femininity		
	Neutrality		
Being male or female biologically	**Sex**		
	Male		
	Female	Also on a biological scale	
	Intersex		
How you behave when turned on	**Creation**		
	Varies, but let's use the Big 5 personality, 2 interpersonal categories, and 3 scopes of focus		
	Openness to new experience	**Warmth** vs **coldness**	**Self**-focus
	Conscientiousness regarding rules	**Dominance** vs **submission**	**Other**-focus
	Extraversion		**World**-focus
	Agreeableness		
	Neuroticism (opposite of **emotional stability**)		

People who change sexes are (linguistically at least) transsexual. People who change gender are (linguistically) transgender, even though we often use "transgender" to describe a transsexual change, and "gender" to describe sex. Because public organizations are squeamish about using the s- word in anything.

I tell people when you read the above table from top to bottom, you get a pretty good summary of who you are and what you like. I'm an [s-poly hetero alpha feminine male] who prefers warm, neurotic, world-focused women as co-creators. Just knowing a line like this can save a person a lot of time and effort sifting through potential mates. Because I'm alpha, I like submissive-style partners, but I'm also feminine in polarity so I don't like to dominate. My biologically trained male dominance is directed strongly, fiercely towards my work in the outside world, not in my relationships at home. So having a feminine "world" at home balances me greatly. My best relationship feels less like we are one man and two women in our society's giggly notion of physical harem, and more like we are three women in deeply intellectual mission.

In finding our place, I also like to have people go down the table four times:

- once for **themselves**
- once for **who they seem to be** in the eyes of the people they naturally attract
- once for the kinds of **partners** they've traditionally attracted
- and once for the kinds of **partners they actually prefer.**

It looks like this:

Person	Number	Gender	Polarity Preference	Polarity	Sex	Creation when turned on

Who attracted people think I am or who others expect me to be	mono	hetero	alpha	masculine	male	less conscientious
						uninhibited {
						    open
						    extraverted
						    agreeable}
						warm
						dominant
						other-focused (on her)

Actual Me	s-poly	hetero	alpha	feminine	male	conscientious
						technical {
						    non-open
						    non-extraverted
						    disagreeable (picky+)}
						warm+
						world-focused+ (on the trio)

Who I attract	mono	hetero, bi	alpha	masculine	female	pleasure-seeking {
						    open, less conscientious
						    self-focused}
						critical, argumentative {
						    extraverted
						    disagreeable
						    dominant}

Partners I actually prefer	poly	bi	beta	feminine	female	artistic hedonistic {
						    open+, conscientious
						    warm and neurotic
						    agreeable and self-focused}
						controlled receiver {
						    non-open, exacting (neurotic)
						    conscientious
						    cold yet caring {
						        (other- or world- focused
						        based on others' needs and
						        submissive)}}

Some people may think making a chart of their preferences is weird, but it's no different than filling out a dating profile and letting the site chart it for you. I noticed that when I made this chart for myself not only did I have to clarify what I wanted for myself (not just producing a gee whiz moment on a website) but I also got to look at those places where the expectations were clearly mismatched. I marked these with an X. While there exists this expectation that I as a man should be dominant, your dominance becomes tricky when your mate insists on dominating *you* to get it to happen. All that is is oppression. I learned that this was a large part of the reason I've ended up having so few males, masculine, and alpha types among my friends. It's a fine trait, but not forced on me.

I also had to accept that I liked conscientious, neurotic women (in the personality-test sense, not the crazy sense). That is, women who have a certain area of expressive focus where they become nonsensically, intractably obsessive. I've found that the women in my life who don't have this still have the socially-trained ego intractability, but it's undirected. Many expect their mate to direct it for them. But that's not my job. This is one of those areas where you like something you're trained to not like, so you lie to yourself about it and attract people who lie to themselves about it too.

Ultimately as an s-poly, I am deeply in love with the interplay of art and society. Society is cold and functional; art is living and colorful. Without each other, though, neither has a foundation to stand on. My artistic hedonist and controlled receiver produce a gorgeous dynamic in which each is able to reach dizzying heights in their natural expression—the structuring society which submits chained to its own volcanic inner stirrings, the artistic wonder which splashes its art selfishly across every inch of society's walls.

And I am only a passive actor. I see a pattern and sometimes wish to take part in it, sometimes wish to extract the excessive combinations of deeper possibility from it. My traditional upbringing didn't teach me how to do this, but failed trained-relationships showed me clearly that the process needed to be explored. Every moment with my Princess and Lover—even if it's just doing chores at home—is an opportunity to exchange with a world that supports all that I wish to be. I support them in turn. Knowing our sexualities makes understanding that creative terrain much easier.

14 DIMENSION 2: *This is Me*

Rarely do we think of the co-creative process as a part of something larger. We're so used to considering sex as the main event that it often doesn't occur to us that our sex life is only a part of who we think we are. One of the great joys in life, for some, is the journey of self-discovery. Unfortunately, for a lot of us self-discovery stops in middle school and high school. There our responses to things become so crystallized that our subsequent years in education and the workforce tend to serve as reaffirmations of our earlier years.

You may be thinking, "I definitely changed after high school." Of course you did. We all have. But in terms of how we label ourselves and allow ourselves different perspectives, our lives rarely change outside of the new relationships we adopt. Becoming a parent, finding our true circle, and identifying with a broader social stance each qualify as life changers, but most of what these build on is accomplished while we're still in school learning the social ropes. For those major events like parenting and family loss, the ways in which we identify ourselves are more sparsely modified.

So what do the school of life and self-discovery have to do with sex? These tell us what we bring to the table when we enter a sexual relationship. Am I your husband or your friend, your partner or your lover? Despite surely having multiple roles at once, I'll tend to have a primary family of roles in life in general, and sex with you is one of the ways in which I support or deny those roles. Throughout the years I've found that an overwhelming percentage of the people I've met don't know themselves, don't know what they want out of life, don't know what they're best at giving back to life, and lean on their relationships to define these things for them. So we'll need to talk about that kind of sex which takes place completely within our identities alone. Get ready for something new. Dimension 2 is all about celibacy.

Right after a long-time relationship ended for me a few years ago, I picked up Elizabeth Abbot's *History of Celibacy*. It was a brilliant work chronicling the lives of people who chose to abstain from sex temporarily or over the long term, and how such abstention was very often associated with either 1) inner power or 2) contact with a higher outer power. There were people building communities, following the calling of faith, creating enterprises, and excelling in sports—geniuses and skill masters of all kinds. After finishing the book, I decided to enter on a three-year commitment to celibacy myself. The deal was sealed, and three years later I had made it through without falling off the wagon. Over the course of the years I observed that there were three kinds of celibacy: normal celibacy in which you didn't have sex with anyone, strict celibacy in which you didn't have sex with yourself either (including masturbation and orgasm), and very strict celibacy in which you didn't indulge sexual stimulation of any kind—with others, with yourself, or in the thoughts and environments you surrounded yourself with. Mine was the second kind, strict celibacy, and it changed me dramatically.

Celibacy

During my strict celibacy, I continued to do porn for research, continued to go through intense sexual phases, and continued to be sexually stimulated (though not in the intercourse sense) in all kinds of ways. I discovered I was polyamorous, that I leaned towards Dom in relationships, evolved a friendship circle almost entirely of intelligent women, wrote three books on astrology and started a business. I'm a very happy person today with a heavy sense of self-efficacy and self-possession, and if you ask me where this all started I'd tell you it was during my celibacy years. The irony of these years was that I had more turbulent relationships with girls than ever during this time because I became so open with my thoughts under zero threat of failure, so that when I told a girl she was sexy for example, she would think that I was hitting on her. *Nope, just observing what to me is a fact. I say it to anyone to whom it applies.* All told, the celibacy years essentially comprised those classes in SELF101 where I learned with certainty what my worth consisted of and what my identity was built on.

Many people think that celibacy is hard. Maybe it is if you're used to having and enjoying the physical company of another to fulfill your biological needs. But if either the having or the enjoyment is missing from that equation, and if you honestly feel that your co-creative relationships are not getting you where you want to go in life, celibacy will not only be easy, but it might very quickly become a point of pride for you. By the end of year one I was proud of the discipline I had developed—the ability to explain to myself *why* that girl wasn't what she pretended to be, *why* that woman would not support my life path despite supporting my body. Celibacy is only hard when you think that your animal need requires animal action of a specific kind. But often during those years I would go through phases of horniness that topped the charts. Moods like that are funny because they really put a signature on your Dimension 12 vibe, inviting others to approach you with their Dimension 6. The hornier I got, the more charming I became, the more women I attracted, and since there were no plans to jerk off anytime soon, all I could do was let it burn for three years. Celibacy of the strict kind teaches you how to seduce with your energy rather than with your actions. Normal celibacy teaches you how to rely on yourself without a partner. Very strict celibacy teaches you how to thoroughly police your mind.

So what is there to say about non-sex besides the fact that sex isn't had? Not much *unless* we explore the kinds of things a celibate person does when sex presents itself as a possibility. That's when celibacy gets interesting. When you have the co-creative impulse floating around you, but have decided not to exercise it through the body, there are alternative routes that you will almost certainly have to take in order to keep that energy from piling up in you. One of the first things a recently celibate person learns is that the best time to halt a sexual pile up is either at the very beginning or just before the very end of the stimulant. I tried for a couple of months to start what I knew I wanted to be strict celibacy before actually starting, but would keep falling out of it into masturbation before I finally worked out a mental play book for avoiding this. From then on during the actual three years I would have a pretty thorough array of responses for directing that intensity elsewhere. Sometimes I'd stop the impulse at its onset, but most of the time I'd just let that hot chick turn me on with her talk anyway, then go do something else when the encounter was over. Celibacy doesn't have to feel like murdering babies. All it is is doing something else.

What you do in place of sex when the sexual urge hits you constitutes the central focus of a celibacy period. Remember,

- Celibacy is unpartnered (controlled Earth)
- Strict celibacy is unreleasing (controlled Fire)
- Very strict celibacy is unstimulated (controlled Water)

so the whole point of celibacy *is* to experience the co-creative rush so that you can send it elsewhere—to your own Earthy company, to specific Fiery actions, or to specific Watery wants. It's not really about having all the potential booty around you go away. That's more like starvation. Instead, the whole point is to investigate your own biologically solo potential when a shared potential might otherwise be the go-to option. You won't be leaning on another to distract you. In the two cases of strict celibacy you won't have depletion of your energy as an option (you'll have to do something with it). In the case of very strict celibacy you won't have an external source as emotional fuel—only yourself and your Rule Set. But before you go thinking that one form of celibacy is superior to the other I'd like to emphasize that the impulses you choose to direct will depend on your unique identity.

Celibacy may not even be for you. If your current path in life is one where you really are tasked to co-create experiences through deep exchange with a partner, it might be much better for you to go forth and multiply, fuck like rabbits, or have as many orgies as you want. That's your path. If that path changes and you really need to figure out how to co-create with your better self as your only partner, then a period of celibacy might do you some good. General celibacy, strict, and very strict can each show you different aspects of that co-creation, and really teach you the actual behavioral packages you prefer in their respective realms independent of another person. People don't generally do celibacy to punish themselves. From what I gather on this seldom-discussed topic, they typically do it to empower themselves and to free themselves from certain kinds of bullshit previous relationships have handed them. (That's why I did it.)

Celibacy on a Timeline

Let me urge you the reader to give Dimension 2 a try to see what you find about yourself. Don't worry, it'll be easy. And here's why:

Just like regular sex, celibacy shouldn't (in most people) be expected to go on forever. Just like regular sex, intentional celibacy has a set window where you're paying attention to the fact that you're doing it. The rest of the time it's not even a thing on your mind. So in order to really get empowered by celibacy, it will be <u>essential</u> (for most of us normal people) to set a stopping point for it. You wouldn't realistically want to jump in the bed and fuck nonstop for the rest of your life, and unless you're on a more involved spiritual or expressive path you wouldn't want endless celibacy either. For most of us that wouldn't be fair to the universe full of potential partners whose lives we could truly enrich through sex. Set a stopping point. If you get to the stopping point and you want to keep going, set a new stopping point after that.

One of the things that I found most unfortunate in *History of Celibacy* were those stories of people who started celibacy, slipped, then beat themselves up for it. They saw it as a broken commitment, a failure, and I think that's so sad. Cars need fuel. Animals need to mate. At least in terms of nature, you shouldn't beat yourself up for sharing pleasure with someone else or yourself. That's our animal fuel. A good way to set yourself up for disappointment is to enter celibacy without an end point. You have no idea if you're going to meet the love of your life next month. There's no need to do that to them or yourself. I chose three years because that was a long enough window to be meaningful (it was actually NOT to challenge myself) and because it was the longest window of time that I could conceive for making a perfect partner wait if I met her the next day. It would compel us to spend time knowing and trusting each other first, as well as assure me that she had the capacity to consider my priorities in the same way I know I would consider hers. I ran into a lot of hypocritical, fuck-it-now types of women during my three years, and am grateful to myself for having set up a system for easily filtering these selfish types out. That's what celibacy does for you. It separates the real co-creators from the object-seekers.

> One simple suggestion for your celibacy is this. Your window should be long enough to serve as a meaningful accomplishment for you, not so short as to be just your regular non-sexual cycle, and not so long as to inconvenience any future, quality relationships.

Your window will likely be different for different types of celibacy, and the types of celibacy you embark upon or not will depend on what you're trying to gain for yourself. Since I love studying sex, psychology and data and, more importantly, am very happy with my subconscious space, I don't see myself doing very strict celibacy any time soon because I don't need it. If I set a window for it at all it might be one day. I also love women's company a lot, so I couldn't even tell you what a window for normal celibacy might be. Strict celibacy, however, appeals to me a lot. I could be in a sexless relationship and be very happy (most Dimension 12 exchanges work this way), and since I'm often interested in seeing what new actions I could accomplish on my own, I might set another year-long window whenever. That's how the timeline process works. Despite what it looks like and how I defined them, the three kinds of celibacy DO NOT STACK, and you can practice any one of them without practicing the other two. The Essenes as a religious community, for example, could be described as displaying very strict celibacy and strict celibacy without the normal type, because the camaraderie will have been so viscerally close. Actually, let me talk about this.

During celibacy, it is still possible to have other kinds of sex. Normal celibacy + sexting is one obvious example. A monk might say you were cheating if you did this, but who gives a shit what he thinks? It's your development, not his. Another example is that of strict celibacy + Dimension 12. This was the kind I followed. In general, the best sexual supplements to non-sexual celibacy lie in Dimensions 12, 10, and 4— Sleepwalking, Limits, and Inclinations respectively—because these dimensions each operate on limited or hidden exposure of the normal biological mechanisms involved: they constitute sex in the mind and not necessarily on the body. Dimension 10 (and Dimension 11 after this) are especially rich with all kinds of fascinating and wonderful ways to fill yourself with fuel without dumping that fuel on someone else's privates. The aim during celibacy is to do stuff, not to NOT do stuff, so there's a good chance some people might still seek out tits and dicks after all. They won't build children with these, though. With the relational passions they've worked on redirecting, they might build businesses.

Discipline is the name of the game when you're celibate, and like so many things this is easier to pull off if you keep your mind on what you're after rather than on what (or how) you're trying to block. Leave the baseball team at home. Focus on the prize.

Say Thank You

In the space between formal relationships, many of us automatically adopt the thought "It's too bad I can't find the right person." But as we've seen so far, our world is positively full of partner-style dynamics at any moment. The things we brag about, the ways in which we play, and the work we do for others are all ways in which we engage interactants, and when we decide to recruit our bodily impulse as part of a co-creative process in these realms, we color these realms with experiences analogous to the sexual. It's not necessarily the case that an unpartnered person is automatically a Dimension 2 person any more than a power-wielding person is automatically a Dimension 8 person. It *is* the case though, that being *unwillingly* unpartnered, an "incel" or its equivalents, presents a ripe opportunity for Dimension 2 exploration. When we want to be partnered but aren't, when we want to co-create but think we can't, we have all the conditions in place for **Dimension 2**: what we'll now call **Identity Sex**. This is co-creation with your better self—or, if you like, your potential "effect-package" on others—as partner.

I really don't like to think of solo sexuality as having sex with myself, so as a straight male I prefer to conceive of a kind of optimum feminine counterpotential to my male physical body as my co-creator. We're going to dive into the scientifically-spiritual for a second so follow me:

Back in Dimension 5 I noted how the 17 factors we used to translate from play to sex were drawn from different sources in psychological research. One those sources was a two-axis sexuality model, the Bem Sex Role Inventory or BSRI. In interpersonal research, humans have long been found to behave along two basic axes, communion (getting along) and agency (getting ahead). The BSRI allows us to take the getting along axis and assign it to stereotyped femininity training while we assign the getting ahead axis to stereotyped masculinity training. Crossing these two axes gives you a kind of playing field for measuring where a person puts their priorities in sex-typed exchanges. The four directions that result are 1) getting along, 2) anti-getting along, 3) getting ahead, and 4) anti-getting ahead. Even if you are a stone cold rock of a man's man (getting ahead), there will be a place on these axes which indicates your opposite (anti-getting ahead). So if your man-hobby was, say, punching faces, your opposite would be the type of personality that likes to get its face punched. You can imagine how, even though you like punching faces, you also like—even need—this other kind of personality in order to conduct your business properly...

...Okay man's man, so what happens in your downtime? You're not actively assaulting people, but you still have the capacity to. Now your getting ahead has become a *potential* rather than a current reality. This version of you isn't attacking anyone, just sitting on the couch with his agent. Despite your normal emphasis on getting ahead, you're now getting along. This is your complement—a side of you which is who you would be if you lived in the alternative interpersonal role (femininity). Your agent would be your anti-complement—the opposite to your complement.

Just as we have four elements that we've used to describe us throughout the book, we also have four overall expressive versions of ourselves: us, our interaction space, potential us who's not us right now, and its potential interaction space which is not such a space right now. The connection to the four elements isn't an accident; you can see these as Fire, Earth, Air, and Water respectively. Readers into math may recognize this as 1, -1, i, and $-i$ in the complex plane, and this is more of a byproduct of things that follow a cycle than it is just spiritual mumbo jumbo. The spiritual part, however, comes from the definition of spirit we used earlier in the book. Spirit was the "extra information" associated with you when you're removed from the picture. Going back to our man punching faces, his "potential" would include the version of him which exists when he's doing something other than that. Also recall how we talked about "potentializing" in the body parts chapter—the stories people tell of you once you leave. This all shows how we really do have multiple selves:

- who we express ourselves as (action, us, Fire, getting ahead, and—for normally, external-world-socialized women—getting ahead by getting along / action through what is communicated)

- what we're identified with (identity, our interaction space, Earth, anti-getting ahead, and—for normally, external-world-socialized women—anti-getting ahead by anti-getting along / identity through pattern of wants)

- who we're attempting to be (communication, our intentions, Air, getting along, and—for normally, external-world-socialized women—getting along by anti-getting ahead / communication through the interaction spaces they keep)

- and what we're trying to identify with (wants, our potential interaction space, Water, anti-getting along with what's already there, for normally, external-world-socialized women—anti-getting along by getting ahead / wants through the pattern of actions)

Perhaps you can see how women's dynamics are just a rotation of men's dynamics where men are assumed to be the standard. When we assume women to be the standard, the rotation happens again.

Multiple selves: Women as the standard

- who we express ourselves as (action, us, Fire, getting ahead, and—for normally, internal-world-socialized men—getting ahead by what they see as anti-getting ahead / action through the interaction spaces / surrounding activity they maintain)

- what we're identified with (identity, our interaction space, Earth, anti-getting ahead, and—for normally, internal-world-socialized men—anti-getting ahead by getting ahead / identity through their actions)

- who we're attempting to be (communication, our intentions, Air, getting along, and—for normally, internal-world-socialized men—getting along by anti-getting along / communication through the wants or emotions they express)

- and what we're trying to identify with (wants, our potential interaction space, Water, anti-getting along with what's already there, for normally, internal-world-socialized men—anti-getting along by getting along / showing wants for things through their choice of communication)

If you're single and want to better understand the opposite sex, look at the <u>potential</u> effects of how you plan to behave towards them, not at your plans themselves. There's a really good chance things will work out exactly as you expect. This is especially good knowledge when you need a way to kill a relationship without getting your hands dirty, because you can essentially get the other person to do things in response to acts you never performed. The other person may end up hating you, but you won't hate yourself. And that's what matters.

Getting back to the idea of multiple selves, when you undertake the identity-building process with "nobody" as a co-creator, you as the Air person getting along will enter a dialogue with any of your three other kinds of self:

- Fire-You: your potential actions as accessed through strict celibacy

- Earth-You: your real interactant-space of things or people you should truly identify with, met through normal celibacy

- Water-You: your truest and best-matched wants and inclinations as trained through very strict celibacy

Just as you think of yourself as a self and not as a bag of atoms, you can think of these other characters as other selves. And even if all of these are just other versions of you, you can still interact with them as though they were of a sex other than yours. Why would you want to do this? It's hard for me to capture this for you in words. I will tell you that it feels more like talking to guardians or guides who actually care about you this way, and those of us who really love to receive affection may be MUCH more successful in their journey doing things like this. In my meditations I have a male Air soul, but the voice that pushes me towards being a better person is a very lusty, Fiery female. If you like, you can think of it as an internal monologue with characters you've called in to counsel you.

The additional benefit in talking to a potential-you or a potential interactant of you who has your preferred-partner's sex is that it may be a lot easier to offset any frustration you have with being unattached. You could go out and squander your precious energy on those dating jerks, or you could go home and augment your talents under the steady encouragement of an ideally forward projecting context (a.k.a. masculine potential space). Don't knock it till you try it, especially if you have any belief in other kinds of spirits at all.

If you think this is weird by the way, Dimensions 3 and 11 may challenge you quite a bit.

In response to being unwillingly single one of the best things you can do is say Thank You. When you were in that last relationship, maybe it was no good. Or maybe it's future wasn't so promising. Whatever the case, it's now just you and your world full of platonics, flirts, and bffs. You're stuck with your own beautiful body, stuff you like to experience, and events you can control. You're able to look in the metaphorical mirror and practice drawing out of yourself the same kind of time-resistant self-possession as those grannies in Dimension 10. Say what you want about people like that, but they're surely bolstered by something enduring that most of us may never come close to accessing. Are you that comfortable in your own skin yet? Your time unpartnered, celibate or not, is your time to make yourself more useful to people besides yourself...by making yourself more useful *to* yourself. Dimension 2 presents you with at least three options for doing this.

Gathering Your Findings

The good thing about Dimension 2 is that it's one of the few dimensions that lends itself to a tangible goal. My goal when I started celibacy was to become as powerful as the people I had just read about and come to admire. My quest for inner power was answered through the people I met and the projects I took on. When you set a goal for this dimension—to love yourself, to be better to others, to get over your fears, or discover who you are—you'll tend to return to this goal more and more easily as you get used to your time without distractions. People in longer-lived relationships who need to figure themselves out can also benefit from Dimension 2. A week or two without sex. A day without stressors. Even a day or two of silence can open your eyes to certain things. And yes you *can* do silence if you have a partner who is understanding enough. I had an awesome three-day affair which started on day 2 of my second day of mute silence; we all met while I was still in no-talking mode (the L, J, memory from the Dimension 5 chapter). It can be done. And the uniqueness of events like this make them all the more memorable (and conducive to much greater appreciation of the partner who let you do this without forcing you to break your commitment).

By the time you get through your Dimension 2 window, you might find noticeably more clarity in how you identify yourself. "I am the oldest," "I am a leader," "I have a sharp eye for talent," "I love and deserve respect," "I enjoy writing," "Design is my passion." These are just some examples of how you might describe your true preferred interaction space to others once you've found out what that space is. While in Dimension 2, you may not be having physical sex. You may or may not have a partner. But you will definitely be a co-creator alongside a force that matches your best path. It's up to you to use this time wisely.

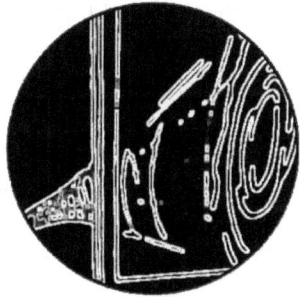

15 DIMENSION 11: *A Unique Society*

Wherever you go, there is information to be passed. The birds have places to go, the bugs have other bugs to see. The computers have networks to talk to. And the people have expectations to share, observations to make. These are the worlds we surround ourselves with whose defining feature is the traffic that gets passed across them.

Back in Dimension 9 we saw how we were able to plant a seed in the bigger world for having that world remember us. Here in Dimension 11, the soil in which that seed was planted will now reveal itself. Though society is shared, our place in it colors that society through our lens. This makes us right at home in the talk that surrounds us...no matter how pleasant or unpleasant that talk seems on the surface.

Natural rebels attract shocked faces. System designers attract disorder. Caretakers attract the assaulted. There is a solid place in each of our lives for the kinds of dynamics we're made to grab onto. A typical information space will consist of at least three main actors: the source of the information, the receiver of the information, and the witness to the dynamics between these first two. In your world you're typically the witness, and the dynamic with which your personality is most strongly associated will present you with a minimum of two basic forces: the one that irks you and the one that attracts you. If you think back to Dimension 4, you'll recall how we took the time to expose some of your less friendly forces and include them into your subconscious fantasy plan. Dimension 11 is where such forces live in the real world, so that the kinds of irritants you listed in Dimension 4 will constitute one half of the normal cast of characters in Dimension 11.

The other half of your Dimension 11 character pool comes from the set of people who called on you in Dimension 6. Remember that group of people who kept asking you to do things you weren't necessarily in the mood to do? Those individuals against whom you were constantly working to maintain common ground? Now they have returned. And there are a lot of them. You can't just help them all. Or can you? You can't just tell them all to go away. But should you invite them? So much of it depends on how effective you think you are as a source of unique expression. The more you believe in your own ability to contribute to these Dimension 6 people's lives, the more opportunities you'll seek to give them a hand in their never-ending struggle against those fiends in Dimension...7?

Dimension 4 may have had some irksome characters in it, but that's only because this was the chapter where we asked about such characters. Dimension 7, however, actually describes the mechanisms that those "enemy groups" in Dimension 4 employ. None other than our old friend persona, the Lovemaker. Oh my! How is it that the social information around you is actually an ongoing story between your Duty calling style and your One-on-one feedback style? It's actually pretty simple. You have a psychological framework for communicating with another for fun, and a framework for what has to be done. You like to see a job well done lead to a good connection, dimensions 6 → 7. But when this pair travels in the other direction—connected communicators creating work that now needs to get resolved (7 → 6)—there's a psychological sense of these "reverse communicators" undoing what you just did—what you were *designed* to do even! How could they? Those villains, them! It bugs you to no end that there are people out there, countries out there, companies out there who would take your heartfelt Dimension 6 → 7 service and mockingly turn it into 7 → 6 disorder. So you declare these un-7s the enemy and surround yourself with the soap opera of theirs and your peer-6's rivalry. That's the central theme in your Unique Society. Your Dimension 11 is an approximation of this story.

If you think about the shows you watch or the music you *prefer* to listen to, you may notice that they seem to reflect a consistent group of plots. The plots usually involve an issue that needs resolution, and a certain kind of character—human or otherwise—which resolves them. There is usually a system (World), a group (Other), or a personal situation (Self) which serves as the perpetuator of the issue, and we'll call that the antagonist. In the entertainment you surround yourself with, the resolver of the issue might be an individual or might not be. A history buff might see certain battle *tactics* (a World) as the hero. A biology fan might see a *process* as the hero (another World). Traditional movies might have singular heroes (a Self) or a combined team which is stronger together as the hero (Other) and all of these aspects combined tell you something about how you believe your grand gathering of interactors to work with each other. If you like several kinds of entertainment with many different kinds of plot structures (as most of us do) then the Self-Other-World characters of the 6-Hero-Resolver and the 7-Antagonist-Disorderer will tell you about certain subdimensions of your overall Dimension 11 story.

Perhaps you can see here how a social story can be thought of as imposing a 12-dimensional Resolver's intention onto a 12-dimensional Disorderer's loved space, taking place in a 12-dimensional setting. This is just like the translation from hobby to interaction style in Dimension 5. It turns out that your perfect Dimension 5 has as its social surroundings, your Dimension 11. So if you want to know what your ideal social talk world looks like, all you need to do is go back to what you wrote down in Dimension 5 and see which of your preferred movies, shows, or other kind of entertainment it matches:

Take your conclusion from Dimension 5 and pick a show, movie or other source of entertainment (that you like following) which roughly matches that conclusion plot-wise.

I know this is technical, but stay with me here. You'll like where we end up.

Once you have your matched entertainment source, think about which of the previous dimensions we've talked about best matches your favorite sexual mode. This dimension is analogous to that aspect of the entertainment you should look to recreate in your work for the social world. We're saving Dimension 3 for last because it's one that you won't have to think too hard about in this process, but if you really really like communicating your inner thoughts and opinions to people above all else then 3 will be your dimension. You can also pick several dimensions if several are your favorite. Once you have your favorite dimensions, you can put everything together to create a world.

Social story element	Your answer
1. Our created world begins with the one we're currently in: The Villains' World. Describe this in terms of its Dimension 7 (according to your view). Is it confusing, angry, entitled, or full of betrayal? Or maybe the communication is great, just that there are still too many poor out there. Here the Villain would be Poverty. Maybe communication is great, but there is so much still to be discovered. This is The Yet-to-be-Discovered as the Villain. Write down your villain to the right.	

Dimension 11: Sex to Defy Others' Boxes

2. Next, write down your Dimension 5-matched show or entertainment item.	
3. Take some space to describe what you like about this show.	

4. List your favorite dimensions among the 12—ones you have the most interest in. Here's a key to help you:

1. How it brings out your instinct, how it shows the untamed instincts of others	5. How entertaining it is, how it excites you	9. What to brag about or broadcast
2. What you associate it with, how it affirms what you think of yourself	6. How it helps or educates you, how insightful or informative it is	10. The rules it follows
3. How the characters express themselves, how it inspires you to convey your opinions	7. How the characters interact or how you interact with it	11. The story
4. How it makes you want certain things, how the characters play	8. How powerfully it affects you, the use of	12. The mood or setting

out their wants	power in it		
5. Pretend you have the opportunity to put yourself in a setting like the above. Using only the dimensions you preferred, describe what this setting needs to include. If the dimension you're looking at revolves around an aspect you couldn't normally see in real life, include "Insight into..." as part of the description. For example, one of my favorite dimensions was 6, and my chosen show often focuses on the villains' self-defeat. But in real life I usually don't see my opponent's self-defeat in action, so I would put "Insight into the opponent's problems." (If you need to pick another entertainment item which is easier to do this for, go ahead.)			
6. In a situation analogous to box 3., you would ideally belong in an information world in which you used box 5 to undo the work of box 1. Now go back to the Dimension 10 chapter. If you see any limits which you think are relevant to how this kind of plot line works, list them to the right. Don't list the fetish, just the limits. These are the specific situations that your ideal world will need to either use (✓) or resolve (✗).			

The above boxes constitute the core of the information world that surrounds you. To create a life for yourself which is *as* entertaining as the entertainment you consume, you can use the steps above to shape your context. Actually, you probably do this already. But if you didn't know, now you know. And if you haven't owned this script yet, you might not have achieved as much of a place in the broader world-story as you would ideally want.

Please Forgive Me

Again there are four major actors in your world story. Heroes, Villains, Bystanders/Settings, and Plot Flows. Don't expect to call on the bystanders. You may spend a considerable part of your life learning who the villains actually are. Recognizing the plot flows requires that you do some self-discovery. And your fellow heroes have all of these same problems. Because of all this, it's actually very rare to see a person really move beyond his familiar informational context in order to contribute positively to the world he has interpreted. Instead, most people simply accept everybody in the story as friends, fr&nds, or people who piss them off. Also, they usually don't take the time to learn enough about their plot flows to clarify their own contribution to it. When you're finally ready to accept your role in interpreting the world you've interpreted, and you're ready to take the needed measures to establish your better self in that world, you'll also be ready for a co-creator to supply you with tools to rewrite the very foundations you're standing on. That co-creator may be a physical partner or a Dimension 2 version of yourself, but make no mistake about it, there will be a shakeup. There will be talk. There will definitely be an episode to remember as your friends, lovers, and homies see their roles all scrambled up. But you'll need to be ready to displace them. Ask the world you knew to forgive your coming nonconformity. You're now ready for Dimension 11 sex.

The basic premise of **Dimension 11** sex is simple. It's the kind of sex you have when you want to say, "Fuck this world. I want that world." The co-creators who travel with you in this kind of sex know you're up to no good in *somebody's* eyes, and they don't care. They're world-writers with you. It's not necessarily that you're doing anything outlandish, it's just that you're using sex as a tool to defy a very broadly executed pattern in the world you conceive. Although 11's astrological equivalent Aquarius isn't always about defiance, in the sexual case where we're <u>creating something new</u> on top of a stable world we already know, defiance in the eyes of at least some of that world's occupants is generally what happens. Accordingly let's call this situation **Defiance Sex**.

Dimension 11 co-creation works against a system you've encountered, not an individual. It's not revenge sex (8 or 1) or show-off sex (9). In working against that system you and your co-creator set up new norms for the way communication is expected to happen, and while you're at it you typically make a statement to any of several types of key characters in your regular social world. There is an emphasis on key characters here because random strangers usually don't count unless their weigh-in becomes a thing to you. So if society thinks gay is not okay today but is okay tomorrow, then same-sex coupling would be considered defiant today but not defiant tomorrow. In other words, you really need to have norms *that exist* in order for Dimension 11 to happen, and at the very least you and your partner need to do things that challenge, undercut, or modify those norms. This is the key to Dimension 11: challenging norms in your social information world— **especially the norms of your un-7s.**

As we saw earlier in the world construction scenario, un-7s are those people in your world who use the same communicative tactics you use, but use them to undo the kind of work that you normally do in your personal duty patterns. There's a lot you can learn about what your un-7s want, but most of what you need to know you already practice through your work life. My own un-7s use judgment of others to elevate themselves and can be collectively described as "Oppressors of Those Not Like Us." Since my service is System Structuring, my path would be using System Structuring to defy the Oppressors of Those Not Like Us. My co-creator would be anyone with whom I partnered to create something which defied my un-7s in the same way. That's the setup, but not the sexual part.

To have Dimension 11 sex, you and your partner need to DO something which embodies your defiance. The good news is that you probably know full well what this is. It's something you've wanted to do for a while, you're pretty sure you would like, and are pretty sure would make your un-7s or more conservative circle-mates mad. I can't say this for a fact, but I'm pretty sure we all have at least one Dimension 10 thing that we would totally do given the right disinhibiting drug; that thing—if we did it—would constitute a behavioral Molotov through the window of our communicative enemies. My "enemies" (if I had any) would be those who lock others out and oppress them, so my Dimension 11 would involve using system structuring to let marginalized outsiders in and free them. For me that's threesomes and polyamory, fetish-openness and foreigners. If your un-7s liked to produce cheap quality work in response to your skill in high quality creations and your service was Mentoring, your Dimension 11 sex might use Mentoring to produce High Quality work. A maid scene, Master-servant, Daddy & Baby Girl/Stepmother & Stepson, or video capture might be your thing. We won't present an exhaustive list of possibilities here since many are already listed under Dimension 10. Just know that even if you didn't like the Dimension 10 options for owning your own limits, you might still consider those same options for putting limits on the causes you plan to resist.

As for the parallels to your favorite entertainment, the dimensions you associated with your entertainment in the earlier exercise constitute the best context for Dimension 11 sex. In the most generic plot flow,

- your un-7s are the opponent,
- your 6 combined with the thing your un-7s dislike is your tactic against your un-7's,
- your box 5 description is either 1) what you get out of this whole business or 2) the situation you put yourself in in order to get something out of it, and
- your 10 shows the sexual themes which are liberating for you but limiting to your un-7s during this process.
- Your co-creator is your accomplice in all this.

Why Even Go There?

Pleasure aside, there are lots of good reasons to have sex. Recalling how at least one of the reasons for having sex was to please others whether or not it benefitted you, you might see how Dimension 11 serves a similar role as Dimension 6 does. It may seem weird to think that one purpose of your having sex might be to make the world better, but with a little bit of a laugh we might truly say that it is. The worlds we think we live in follow certain rules that we think apply. When we think some of those rules need changing in order to make our perceived worlds run better, one solution is to get undeniable pleasure out of breaking those rules. When you have Dimension 11 sex, you're essentially telling the un-7s in your psychology, "SPLAT. That's what I think of your rules," and you set up a reaction within yourself which robs your un-7s of their power to irk you. Joyous Defiance Sex makes the patterns you defy weaker, if in no other way than reducing their ability to tell you what to do in your own bed. The more we believe that stupid rules can and should be fucked away, the more empowered we feel to resist those stupid rules outside of the bedroom. Strike a blow for freedom. Vote with your pants, not just your hands.

We've discussed some complicated stuff here. All that talk about world-building and entertainment, how is that related to sex again? To summarize,

- Your preferred entertainment captures your preferred information surroundings, including certain communicators in your world who love to undo the kind of work you do as a person: your un-7s. Your un-7s can also be seen in those kinds of people against whom you have a deep-seated bias (from Dimension 4)
- The flow of the stories in your preferred entertainment roughly mirrors the life scenarios which—if you were a character in them—would cause you to be just as entertained by your own life as you are with those folks you're following on the tube. There are parallels between your entertainment preferences and the dynamics in your social information world, so that your conscious views of the former can tell you more about your subconscious views of the latter.
- There are in-the-bed analogs to the kinds of actions you would take to resist your normal cast of adversaries in your social information world, and these analogs are often

Dimension 10-style practices that you've always wanted to do anyway.

- Whatever you choose, Dimension 11 sex <u>is</u> sex against the way you believe things <u>shouldn't</u> be in your social information world. It's not necessarily sex in favor of what you think *should* be.

Finally, let's talk about how you find Dimension 11 partners. In my opinion it's easier for most people to find Dimension 11 partners than it is to find Dimension 10 partners, simply because with Dimension 10 partners you need to agree to put limits on *each other*. In Dimension 11, you join forces to put limits on *some other group*. Also, since the key cast of characters in your life often includes several "fellow heroes" who think like you, it's easy to probe these heroes to see if they too seek to stick it to the un-7s the way you do. It's not a foolproof test, but people whose approach to duty looks like yours and who share more or less the same un-7s you do are more likely to stay with you for a longer time (thanks to the duty part) and defy with you in a similar way (thanks to the un-7s part). All you need to do is watch for these people's existence in your world. You don't even have to probe that deeply...

...The one catch to the above is that your would-be fellow Defiers need to be as interested in *actively* changing their own version of the social information world as you are in changing yours. You're sure to encounter a lot of bystanders who claim to be interested in such things, but will remain comfortably seated on their asses for as long as the status quo lets them do it. The more empowered you are to work against your un-7s for the good of the entire social information space that eternally follows you around, the more easily you'll spot these bystanders. Even if it's in their best interests too, not everyone will have what it takes to join your personal revolution.

16 DIMENSION 3: *It's the Way I Think*

The wildest sex you can possibly have—and the type most people will never get to experience—is not Dimension 1 animal-style, but Dimension 3. When we initially choose partners, we choose them within the bounds of reason, stability, and social order. We go through phases where we learn which things should and shouldn't be said to the partners and when. We don't mind getting physically naked with our partners. We don't even mind getting emotionally naked. But intellectually naked like a frayed myelin sheath? Speaking in alien tongues and talkin' whatever shit strikes you? Who does that? Only partners who know how to let go, my friend, and only partners who've had a really important conversation about it beforehand. We may not be born to be completely honest. We're certainly trained to pasteurize our processes for others' understanding. There's always the sugarcoating, the care, and the intentional wording around those we want to avoid hurting. But these aren't the only ways to communicate during sex.

For the supremely mentally healthy,

For people who completely trust both their partners and, more importantly, themselves,

For those who have seen and accepted their partner's hands-down weirdest traits,

and who aren't afraid to enter stream of consciousness,

For those who love, respect, or at least get along with their partners so deeply that it doesn't occur to them to even hold hurtful thoughts, let alone hide them,

For those who so thoroughly enjoy their partner's body and the feelings that body brings,

For those who are curious to push the edges of communicative sanity in an experience that even they themselves may not ever be able duplicate...

There is Dimension 3.

People who criticize or feel criticized need not apply. People with insecurities or who have partnered with the insecure need not apply. People who have anything to hide at all about themselves or what they think about their partners should save this one for another life, or at least another mate. Dimension 3 is for the communicatively unchained, whose only source of limits are found in their feelings towards the person they're with.

Let's get this out of the way right now. Dimension 3 is the kind of sex you might be able to have on mind altering drugs, but in the drugged case the related Dimension 12 effects won't stay with you, since they'll be inconsistent with who you are undrugged. **Dimension 3** is you all the way. It's sex upon the lines of your truest thinking. That is, **Streaming Sex**.

My one experience with psychedelics was pretty informative. I recorded myself both times, and one day may post those recordings somewhere. My aim was to know what I was like and what kinds of events I would conjure up when my mind was not in a guarded mode. To my pleasant surprise, I talked a lot about love, a lot about how great life is, and a lot about how people need to get off the bullshit and just love each other. I didn't have any worries. None of the things I would have thought would be on my mind—like business, bills, and relationships—were much of a thing. Everything was just blissfully, 1970s-slang, fine. Even though I had been curious to see if any questionable exchanges I happened to be in at the time were going to come up, they didn't. I realized afterwards that deep down I just didn't care to hurt anybody, and thought the idea of doing so was just wasteful of brain. Since then, I trust that I could survive a stream of consciousness exchange with someone who supported that kind of easy bliss. Prior to the psychedelics, I just didn't know. Dimension 3 is not an experience I've had yet, so I can't tell you any more about what it feels like. But I'm tapping the guardians on this one, and here's what they say.

Stream of consciousness sex, or Streaming as you call it is a very simple matter to higher souls. It's like mixing two liquids together. There is little that we have to say about this kind of intercourse, as we believe that a partnership's ability to have it is wholly dependent on the level of trust the partners feel with each other and especially with themselves. We will say that a partnership's ability to have this kind of union is almost always determined from the beginning, and 99.9+% of partnerships in your time and in your population will never be able to have it. They have lied too much to themselves and each other in order to come together and stay together, such that doing this without body-altering substances will be very difficult for them. For those who are genuinely loving and haven't needed to lie to cover their true sentiments regarding things, there is the additional issue of what constitutes normal among their regular circles of influence. This is why we applied the term "lie" to almost everyone. Conformity that stifles the will of those in a relationship given the opinions of those outside of it produces line-following which the actors believe they believe in, but in their spirits care little about. To have an uninhibited union of souls, the trust must be complete, the actors must be ready to rebel against all standards—earthly friends and family included. All actors must be comfortable enough with their bodies and each other's bodies, unafraid of any possible shame or any possible mistakes. And in a little but very important piece of side information, the partners must have demonstrated beforehand that both can forgive the night if things do not go as planned. The bar is high for this one, but if the partners are able to develop the appropriate strength of soul alongside the requisite level of relative disdain for certain norms they see as stifling, this kind of sex will be automatic for the curious. It remains near impossible for the mean. You can take it from here, OML. Namaste.

Thoughts on Dimension 3

You have had streaming sex if:

> Without state-altering substances, consistent with your normal, unaltered, pre-conscious thought and behavioral patterns, you were able to have sex with a partner in which you and your partner were able to say things and make maneuvers which were consistent with the deepest, pre-normed inner monologue they knew themselves capable of having and also conveyed to you.

Both partners. Deepest unfiltered (probably) weirdness. Revealed to each other beforehand. Accepted by each other beforehand. Displayed at will during the act. Words and Maneuvers. No judgment. No fear. No drugs. Full trust.

It's like finding the Ark of the Covenant under your bed.

Knowing that some readers (along with the author himself) have now set this as their ultimate sexual goal after having read about it, I'm prompted to ask 1) what should one truly expect to get out of this and 2) how does one find a person with whom he can do this? It's not like Dimensions 10 or 11; like their nonsexual equivalents Rule and Society respectively, those dimensions have a well-managed framework for us to direct our actions against. Also, in so many ways it's wilder yet more sustainable than Dimension 1; in Dimension 1 you rely on your inner savage to scream your corporeal scream upon the quaking ear of your mate. We typically dilute this with a healthy dose of givin' a shit about the partner's safety and well-being.

With Dimension 3, your primal instinct is anchored to the partner's, so that the two of you go animal together. But it's actually less about animal instinct and more about mutual auto-expression in light of the other, so a fantastically satisfying Other is a must. Because both partners will be conversing in the Stream, the partners will need to have balanced opinions of each other. You can't have one person saying, "Man, you're so hot. You're so sexy" and the other saying "You aight." Or one saying "I love you, babe. It's so...ah...ah...do you love me?" and the other saying "."

It'll ruin the mood probably.

My guess is, the things you get out of the Stream are strongly related to the things you put into it. These revolve around trust, devotion, and a deep acceptance of the kind that no other can give. I'll also guess that the kind of relationship you have to have in order to have this kind of sex and have it *frequently* may be the kind that marries two spirits in the way that no earthly ceremony could. It's one thing to set Dimension 3 as a goal, another thing to set the assorted conditions for *getting* to Dimension 3 as goals. As with so many worthwhile things, the reward in the Stream may not be in the sex itself, but in the path of complete trust you and your partner must travel together to get there.

This brings us to the second question. How do you attract a partner who does this, not for the sexual badge, but as a byproduct of their relationship with you?

I'm pretty certain that you could fake Dimension 3 fairly easily. Possums fake it all the time. We fuck hard, speak a little alien, and roll over dead. Then, when they're not looking, we open one eye and get up to go grab a sandwich. (I've actually done this.) Play a little PlayStation then go home. But that doesn't feel any different than normal Dimension 8 sex with added theatrics. Instead, the key to a genuinely memorable Dimension 3 scene is probably consistency.

We normally turn into someone at least *a little* different in the bed. During Dimension 3 we're the same as always. Accordingly, to find a partner for this is likely a matter of building a relationship with an instantly, no questions asked, attractant for you where faking and posing never enters the relationship as a tactic; you will have known from the very beginning that you wanted to make room for them. Finding them is also likely to be a matter of you being okay with what you know to be the other's quirks, seeing them early and accepting them early. This is where people who are noticeably <u>im</u>perfect in appearance and behavior will have an easier time approaching Dimension 3 than more socially approved people. All of that Dimension 10 discussion of beauty and riches still holds. The more you have, the harder it is to build genuine relationships that aren't made easier by your popularly sought assets. Lastly, finding a Dimension 3 person will likely require a series of informal surveys of your own behavior, in which you notice yourself doing things easily that just wouldn't make sense to do with someone else.

Regarding people towards whom you show a rare trust, there is one person of whom I've said "I want to spend the rest of my life with her." That same person is the only one of whom I've ever said, "I trust her more than I trust myself." She's also the only person EVER where the thought of me losing her over something stupid I did, seriously bothered me every time the possibility came up. I tell you this because this exchange also has some other qualities it may help you in your search to know: She's not a friend, lover, romantic interest, or anywhere close to my default pick for a partner. I don't think it's love, wouldn't quite describe her as a bond, and am not that close to her personally. Most importantly, I wouldn't change any of this and have no compulsion to escalate or update the exchange. She's not a romantic option as far as I can tell, but she's by far the closest to Dimension 3 I've ever gotten—probably because I'm farther along in my own development than I've ever been. I tell you all this because

I'm convinced that as you get closer to finding what you're looking for—a relationship with someone worthy of the Dimension 3 undertaking—you'll find that that person may not remotely resemble all of the superficially trained standards you began your romantic career with. Instead, they'll simply be someone whose path seems— truly on a level beyond this life—tied to yours for the journey.

I wouldn't be surprised if the Rule Set reserved easy Dimension 3 partners only for those who rid themselves of all the barriers to true Dimension 3 trust. I also wouldn't be surprised if these partners only became accessible to those whose capacity to love their potential partner ran so deep that the love itself—much like the Dimension 11 acts—had the capacity to better each partner's worlds. Some relationships, fictional or actual, produce a joint magic which far exceeds the powers of the individuals, or at least outshines the individuals' accomplishments so that more of the world can see it. Marc Anthony and Cleopatra, Romeo and Juliet, Adam and Eve do more for us in their joint stories than they do for us alone. When such joint stories stand to be possible, and the actors therein care so much about each other as to merge their experiences fearlessly into the other's, then Heaven must know: These ones are fit to disclose it all. For those who are already committed, whose options for such openness have already showed signs of a limit, there is still the ability to have a conversation with the partner, "I want to be so much better for you, will you be patient with me as I grow myself?" Conversations like this between people already subject to so many external rules are likely laden with walls and various appeals to the practical, but it never hurts to ask if, for once, it could just be about those two. There is value in giving your partner a week, maybe just a couple of days, to see what it's like to be better if it's possible. The person I described earlier took years for her value to register on my radar. Not because we weren't kindred, but because I (at least) was not past the point of looking for superficialities until a separate and unrelated exchange built on those superficialities failed miserably.

You may not see your truest companion until you stop looking for fake ones. Stop looking for forms and start looking for the dynamics those forms represent. They're already likely to be everywhere in your life. Though gratitude and openness you can see them. By suspending your judgment and ceasing your criticism, by trading your insecurities towards what *might be* for security in what has *always been*, you can stop pushing them away. Like any thought you normally hold, Dimension 3 reflects your pattern for interpreting the events in your life. You can filter those patterns, bolster them with excuses and justifications, and inflate yourself with sentences upon others, but co-creation in that style will never liberate you from the chains those methods really represent. Only by turning your thought pattern into one which is consistently fruitful for those who engage it—including yourself—can you really build a space in which creating with you becomes a complete and fulfilling experience for the other.

And the thing you create together will be better and greater than anything you could have created alone.

Remember, For Dimension 3 sex to occur:

- Build love, safety, honesty, and trust—*in* and *towards* each other.
- Don't worry about what outsiders would say, but cultivate complete, edifying, communicative uninhibitedness in the other and in yourself.
- Make it safe for your partner to show you everything he or she has in her psyche, including their love for you, and let it play out in your co-creation.

17 THE 12 DIMENSIONS

Earlier I claimed that a person wants what they turn their actions towards the experience of. Additionally, let's say that a person **believes** that which he steers his actions around the existence of, consciously or not. Given these mini-definitions, let's present a few more: a person's truest **reason (for a thing)** is that which he believes he [wants], [wanted], [was compelled by], or [was instrumental for] in turning his actions towards that thing.

Now that we have a few ways of looking at our reasons, we can see how a person can not only have many reasons for having sex, but can also retroactively assign himself reasons for having been born into a physical body in the first place. Maybe he was compelled by evolution. Maybe his current personality would have, in his view, wanted him to be who he is. Maybe he now wants to serve his Rule Set. Maybe he is instrumental in his family's history. When he thinks his reasons for being born are attached to a form of his own personality which preceded the one he has in his current body, his current body becomes an incarnation, and his retroactively assigned reasons for being born (even if the original ones are not known) become his reasons for incarnating. To speak of incarnation, we'll need to believe in a form of our personalities or personalized expression which existed prior to the bodies that currently contain us.

Consider your pre-birth self to be a scattering of the nutrients, genetics, parental dispositions and cultures that would ultimately come together to form you—their timeline trajectory aiming towards the gathering point that is you, and you can get a sense of what that pre-birth self might look like. The process of gathering the parts that would ultimately form a thing we'll call **creation**. Anything that served as a reason for that creation will be considered a **creator**. Two or more creators of the same thing we'll call **co-creators** of that thing—especially if they interact directly to do so. Co-creators who are thought to be living, are of the same type, and whose joint process of co-creation involves mutual access of the deepest mechanisms their forms employ for reproducing differentiated others of that same type can be said to possess the capacity for sex. That is, in humans we can consider **SEX** to be the use of our bodies' [co-creative mechanisms for human reproduction] towards the process of co-creation. All of the pleasures, hormones, and bonding states specific to humans are implied. But we don't actually have to create new humans in order for us to qualify as having sex. We only need to use the human-creating mechanisms with another, even if that other is our potential selves. After all, you're just a pattern in my mind. Why can't other versions of me or my fantasies also be a pattern?

We could try to define sex in terms of physical acts, but some people get off just by seeing blood. We could define it in terms of bodily contact, but for some the feather is all they'll get. We could define sex in terms of action, but when two tantrikas can do it by just sitting there holding each other in silence, we realize that none of that matters. Sex is a process we recognize with many other processes which go into it—so that ultimately the goal isn't to get too stuck on a single definition, but to consider the many dimensions that definition might entail. That's what we did in this book, and we produced 12 different approaches to sex:

Dimension (roughly in order of increasing complexity)	Description
8. Classic Sex	Done for a feeling sponsored by the other person or a feeling you want another to feel, actions you want another to perform
7. Lovemaking	Done to engage in continuous feedback communication with how the other *wants* to act or feel *continuously within themselves* (not how they're *compelled* to act or feel by the partner, that's 8)
1. Uninhibited Fucking	Done to release whatever behavioral instincts come to you at any moment
12. Sleepwalking	Done to continue acting even when there is no

	energy left to motivate you to do so
9. Sex for the Image	Done to provide content for the public broadcasting you do towards others
5. Sex for the Play	Done to show your voluntary, obligation-free, expressive preferences towards the target of your voluntary, obligation-free enjoyment
6. Duty Sex	Motivated mainly by the call of another
4. Sex on the Emotional Wants	Done to project the exchanges among inner feelings you wish to send out from yourself
10. Limit Sex	Done to reproduce the limiting or structuring conditions you encounter in life, whether you see these limits as positive or negative
2. Celibacy / Identity Sex	Done to receive sexual input without giving sexual output, while instead redirecting that input into other kinds of creation
11. Defiance Sex	Done to play out your resolution to a class of communication patterns which you naturally and thematically encounter in life and strongly oppose
3. Streaming Sex	Done to play out your uncensored subconscious mind alongside another's uncensored subconscious mind

The more complex the sex, the more "right" you'll have to be with yourself and your partner, and the clearer you'll have to be with your world.

Some Trivia Related to This Book

Even though we've talked a lot about sex, I've found throughout the writing of this book that most of these dimensions are easier to apply towards your non-sexual dealings than your sexual ones. That may be because the co-creative process happens everywhere. An interesting little factoid you might be interested to know is that this current chapter is the last to be written (even after the conclusion), I've written this whole thing from start to finish in just under 80 hours, in 8 days (it's now November 25, 2018), with no outline and no sense of what any of the chapters would contain. I also wrote it almost entirely in some kind of channel or another, along with several cups of vodka and several gallons of tea. Whether or not you believe in guardians, there is truly some force that can get into you and pour through you if you're open enough. Here and in my regular post as a data analyst, I've been doing the most complex work I've ever done as each chapter has appeared, and almost entirely under Dimension 12. (The contents of Dimensions 2 and 6 for me and the social story in Dimension 11 surprised the hell out of me, and although I knew towards the end that Dimension 3 would be something different, I didn't know why. It's been a real joy learning these things as a tool for their creation, and I'm thankful to the guardians for it.) With the exception of Dimensions 8 and 7, the material here has been as new to me as it's being written as it might be to others who read it.

I've now learned that a person's intentional entry into Dimension 2 at some point is almost A NECESSITY for a person to really find his or her creative spark in today's noisy world, that Dimension 3 will definitely be possible for a lot more readers as soon as they find out it exists (especially the younger, more evolved—and frankly more honest—souls), and I've also learned that Dimension 11 is probably the most fun sex you can possibly have (just received that one), and that's probably because—if you like your informational noise—it's the dimension that will restore your power to positively affect that noise where self-promoting media outlets have taken that power from you.

All told, use this book to experiment sexually for sure. But more importantly, do the activities in it (especially the ones under Dimension 4) to truly ramp up your creative spark.

And stop being selfish. Dimensions 6 and 12 will make you spiritually invincible if you master them. (The guardians told me to say that.)

And For Those Who Are Really Interested in Trying the Things in This Book...

For readers wondering why I put all the definitions in this chapter, these—along with this book's definitions for love, beauty, and want—

are the ones I've leaned on <u>heavily</u> to know more clearly what I was looking at over the years' worth of relationships. You may find them important for separating the good from the harmful in your future exchanges, and might especially find them useful for asking how far and in what way you're willing to go with certain people. Use the admittedly formal definitions throughout this book (along with the more technical parts in the beginning) to create sharp divisions among your exchange options. If you do, you'll almost certainly see your self-beneficial intuition increase in every dimension we've talked about—especially 6. *What's my reason for going after this person? Could I actually love this person?* You might have several answers. Now you can more easily decide which ones are worth moving forward on.

You can use the notion of "co-creation" to keep the *real* effects of your relationships nice and obvious to you.

CONCLUSION

During my celibacy years I concluded that polyamory would save the world. Well, maybe not polyamory *per se*, but certainly the cultivation of universal love between individuals, and the development of a culture of openness which, at the very least, made it okay for people to receive love from sources other than their pre-screened social boxes. After a bit more self-discovery, I learned that some people were so into their social boxes that they would actually go to war with you over your giving them goodness. The problem was as clear then as it is now. So many people's protective walls ARE their judgment of others. Breach the wall, get the judgment. Warrant the judgment in their eyes, get the wall. But it is precisely the walls that lock out any additional gifts from being received. When a person seeks their prince or princess but only knows smacking nakedness as proof of the successful attainment of these, we end up with a society whose deepest relationships ride on symbols of love rather than actual love, physical proof of devotion coupled with selective interpretations of the form in which that proof comes. Because we commodify so much of what comes to us, we believe that we must also commodify and measure any gifts life gives to us. But life gives infinitely, so those of us who do this will be infinitely frustrated.

I've had the great pleasure throughout life of having both an unquenchable appetite for love and an inexhaustible love of patterns—chief among those patterns being the classes of human experience. Just prior to writing this book I finally got tired of our country's training in selfishness and decided to move to another, but my guardians reminded me, "You need to write this book." I asked them, *Why me? I'm far from an expert on the subject,* and they told me, "There is a perspective that you have which will benefit people, and those people may not see this kind of information connected in this way for years to come. The world needs more love from more people to each other, but the Western world also needs a reason—proof of that love. It can't be helped, but it can be spoken to. Marry the frameworks that people need, and ask them to pray for something better within themselves and their circles." And so it was.

We tend to think of sexuality as some kind of dark forest. We see the giggling kids go in there; we ourselves have gone; but according to our collective understanding, it's still a dark forest. "There's no way sex could be logically treated in normal people's lives, and no way it could line up deeply with spirituality except in those exotic Indian practices out there." But these are old ways of thinking. We already know that we're packages of energy. We already know that the psychologies about us endure after we're gone, and that these psychologies themselves comprise patterns among our energies—mind as the traffic of brain. While our lives may still be circumscribed by old ways of thinking, we now know enough to see past those old ways. Dogmatic closure just doesn't make sense anymore. It's time to update our views of what we're made of and how the things we're made of take in new influences.

The 12 dimensions discussed in this book are combinations of Self focus, Other focus, and World focus, with four elements corresponding roughly to the four possible directions along the two well-established sociological dimensions of pro- and anti- getting along and getting ahead. These 3 x 4 dimensions have allowed us to look at sex in terms of different experiential agendas, and address many of the psychological corners of these agendas in the process. Despite being commonly trained as a strongly physical, pleasure-anchored process, sex is hardly limited to the physical. We established early on that physical forms are simply atomic ones, and atomic forms are simply energy-carrying ones. Ultimately then, throughout the book, we continually considered form-physical and form-mental things to be energy patterns at their core, and found that analogies across contexts allowed us to keep recycling the same themes for different ends. In this way, sex ceases to be solely about bodies in contact and more about intense exchanges of energy towards the process of co-creation.

Time and again we've seen how the things we do in one domain of experience has effects in another. Ultimately, the process of sex has effects in other domains, so that mastery of those domains helps clarify the sexual constructs associated with them. With this in mind, we moved through the different dimensions roughly in order of increasing experiential complexity, and showed how both the more complex as well as the more fulfilling dimensions required, more than anything, the suspension of judgment and criticism. Judgment and criticism were simply barriers to receiving anything further from sources outside of ourselves.

If sex is to be a safe, intimate, two way affair, then there are aspects of the subject which require that our psychologies and the interactions with other psychologies also be safe ones. Barring this, sex will be limited to the realms of the physical alone, leading us back to the problem of treating everything as a transaction. We want good and pleasurable relationships. We'd like the expected level of sex to come with it. But if we're not willing to make it safe for others to give to us, then we might be asking for too much. Accordingly, each of the dimensions contained its own dose of emotional reality for the one practicing it. There are only so many ways in which you can have good sex or a good relationship without having a good dynamic with partner who cares to provide you with this.

The overall lesson then, is that deep physical intimacy is greatly helped by a healthy, loving psychology. You knew that. But do you practice it?

I hope you've gotten something out of this book, and that it has given you and your partner more tools to build on. By loving each other more truly and more deeply, you reduce the number of needless battles in the world. Take some time to talk to your partner about what he or she wants out of life, then see if you can develop— together—the means for supporting each other on your shared journeys. Don't be afraid to experiment with some new things you may find in that person.

Rightly traveled, your combined path can surely produce experiences greater than either of you could have dreamt of alone. Reassure your partner of where they're headed with you, and receive the love that they and your life itself continually give you.

Conclusion

As an astrologer I would be remiss...

This book's birth time was Saturday November 17, 2018 3:01 am in San Antonio, TX.

I started writing *S12* following a dream in which an auditorium full of strangers, mostly blondes, did a line dance to Manhattan Transfer's version of *Choo-Choo Ch-Boogie*. In that dream a camera I was using exploded. I didn't dance, only observed along with four others.

There was also a dream that I was rushed down a cave's water tunnel, and in the end was asked to jackhammer through the rock ceiling that trapped people for drowning in there. The entrance to the tunnel had initially been pointed out by a person I could have loved years ago, but never did seem to grow past her limits.

www.ingramcontent.com/pod-product-compliance
Lightning Source LLC
Chambersburg PA
CBHW060314030426
42336CB00011B/1048